PRAISE FOR
"AUTISM: TURNING ON THE LIGHT"

"Hindsight is 20/20 and I wish that I had seen a book like this many years ago. I have never encountered anything as informative, inspirational, and heartfelt. Presenting the trials, tribulations, and ultimate success of a child who has Autism in a book through a father's own personal experience is not only unique, but critically needed to serve as a supporting foundation for all fathers and families of children who have Autism. I highly recommend this new and remarkable book to anyone who is experiencing life's journey through Autism."

Karen Parris, Speech-Language
Pathologist, MS Ed., CCC

Recently, a growing amount of attention has come to be focused on a group of disorders called "autism." Researchers continue to more systematically study this phenomenon. Reporting in such publications as the American Journal of Human Genetics, they have broadened their attention to what some have come to call "Autism Spectrum Disorders (ASDs). An increasing number of parents are also beginning to share their personal experiences, their successes, failures, challenges, and even special opportunities in working with these special children and adults. Are there gender-related considerations? Are there school-related considerations? As parent Keith Ambersley, other parents along with other investigators appropriately continue to share their experiences in working with their children or other autistic, our knowledge will increase and our skills will expand for understanding (and when necessary) assisting those who are affected by this rather surprising and unpredictable group of traits called "autism."

Charles Meadows, PhD, Director Center
For Teacher Preparation, Morehouse College

AUTISM:

TURNING ON THE LIGHT

A FATHER SHARES HIS SON'S
INSPIRATIONAL LIFE'S JOURNEY THROUGH AUTISM

KEITH AMBERSLEY

authorHOUSE®

AuthorHouse™
1663 Liberty Drive
Bloomington, IN 47403
www.authorhouse.com
Phone: 1-800-839-8640

Published by AuthorHouse 4/26/2013

ISBN: 978-1-4817-3824-8 (sc)
ISBN: 978-1-4817-3823-1 (e)

Library of Congress Control Number: 2013906554

Dedicated to my son, Aaron Ambersley
YOU INSPIRE GREATNESS
YOU BRING GREAT JOY
YOU ARE SPECIAL
Special acknowledgement to all the special
children their parents and caregivers who do
so much and ask for so little in return!

TABLE OF CONTENTS

Preface

My name is Aaron, and my diagnosis is pervasive developmental disorder (PDD). Generally PDD is readily defined as autism, which is a more recognizable term. This cognitive and receptive disorder prevents me from processing information quickly and accurately with the addition of speech and language delays and attention deficit-hyperactivity disorder (ADHD). I am forced to learn at a slower pace than my peers at school. Everything has to be explained to me at a slower pace so that I can make sense of it all. My dad says it's not important when you get it, but more importantly that you get it!

It's not easy working through the severe learning and development delays that result from autism and ADHD. This duo made it impossible for me to learn and develop academically and interact socially. Today I have an inspiring story to share about how I overcame major speech, learning, and behavior barriers to realize my dreams to learn, have friends, play sports, and grow like any child.

Success for me is defined by the small accomplishments and milestone achievements on my terms and at my own pace. Determination, hard work, and being happy in spite of my multiple delays brought on by autism and ADHD are part of my daily routine. This drives me to work twice as hard so that in the future I can live my life with a reduced form of autism that is less restrictive and more rewarding.

Reading is a dream that has come true for me. I love reading but I cannot write a book or even tell my story in a clear and concise way for you to understand how the path to fulfilling my dream inspires hope for other children and adults with autism and their families all over the world.

My parents work very hard with me. They are patient and continue to emphasize that I can have dreams. Some will materialize, and others will just remain nice thoughts. However, I should not stop dreaming because I have autism which makes me a little different. My dad tells me that where he works they believe in diversity of talents and dreams. That is what makes us all different and special. I am convinced that through love, hard work, time, and perseverance it is possible for me to overcome many of the barriers that have stood in the way of my dreams. Autism challenges me to work twice as hard to realize one dream at a time.

I have many dreams, just like kids without this disability. My ultimate dream right now is that I will get better someday and find a sense of near-total normalcy.

Every day I work very hard to overcome my development barriers, and I work even harder to turn this disability into advancement and growth in pursuit of bigger and better things.

My dreams only become reality through continuous improvement, which I pursue relentlessly on a daily basis. At the end, I want to do the things I like and do them very well. My hope is to do my very best beyond autism. To be recognized for my ability and not for my inability. Most see autism as an insurmountable barrier; I see it as an opportunity for self-improvement.

My dad is writing this book for me to share my story. My story tells of the many obstacles, challenges, and success I've encountered on my journey down the road of autism. I want each parent of an autistic child to realize that no matter how daunting and frustrating the task, nothing is impossible! Each milestone and accomplishment, no matter how small, is a dream realized when put in the right context. I have a long way to go. However, every day leads me closer to realizing my ultimate dream of limiting the autistic restrictions and becoming more independent to the best of my ability.

INTRODUCTION

It is possible, even inevitable, that children diagnosed with autism in the twenty-first century that have benefitted from early intervention and continuous improvement programs will become confident and self-sufficient over the course of their lives. The future is very bright for children with autism when compared to previous generations. Just a couple of generations ago, children who also became adults with autism were subjected to a life of institutionalization stripped of all hope, dignity, and a future. Institutionalization was considered the only option available to families and society trying to politely distance children with autism from personal and social embarrassment.

Today we live in a mature and enlightened society, which wants to be responsible in the way our children and adults with autism are respected and treated. Society is now more progressively responsible for and accepting of children and adults with autism. This change in thinking does not make things perfect for our children, but awareness and treatment are getting better through education, research, awareness, and advocacy. Social change has moved the needle in a positive direction to preserve the right and dignity of children and adults with autism.

As a society we have come a long way with respect to choosing socialization over institutionalization.

This social change is most prevalent in the developed world. In the developing world, this is not always the case due to the lack of awareness, education, shame, and cultural taboos.

Today, in the developed world, children with autism have the right to make choices and gain access to training for skills development that is appropriate for them to live their dreams, exceed expectations, and contribute to society as citizens of their country.

Many private and for-profit companies have either adopted or embarked on a non-discriminatory and inclusive corporate policy. Every day I come across adults with autism actively engaged as employees and members in private companies, corporations, and nonprofit organizations. This is great news for the next generation of adults with autism! However, as parents and as a society, we can all do more to encourage and promote the dreams of our children with autism.

Our family has chosen the path of autism light, which enables and engages our son Aaron so that he can set goals, live his dreams, and exceed his expectations at his pace and on his terms. Wherever his dream takes him, we are right there in his corner to support and encourage him on his journey, to enable him to pursue areas of interest not yet known to us. His dreams could also take him to different countries and cultures. With today's technological advancements and the global community becoming a homogeneous network of people, this dream is both conceivable and possible. In our eyes, autism is not a handicap; it is an opportunity to exceed the human limitations inherited at birth.

All of us do not have equal talent, but all of us should have an equal opportunity to develop our talent.
JOHN F. KENNEDY

As a father of a child with autism, I feel strongly that autism is an once-in-a-lifetime opportunity for me to write about the struggles, challenges, triumphs, and my personal experience about how I have been able to make sense of it. I realize that I have taken so many of my own life-development stages for granted. The skills my son struggles with came so naturally to me.

Putting myself in his shoes, I realize no matter how hard I work on a task, he works twice as hard with fierce effort. Now I have less of a reason to complain about a lot of things in life.

My son is very special, just like every child I meet who has a set of unique needs. He has the desire, drive, and capacity to do great things. First, he has harnessed the capability to overcome great obstacles, and he's not afraid to try harder. It takes something special to live with and overcome autism! Since his birth we have been intrinsically locked on the same journey, a journey that takes us through the challenges and experiences of growing and living with autism. We find ourselves helping each other in so many different ways. He helps me to think outside the box for creative solutions to help him navigate the basic fundamentals of communication and social behavior, which I have taken for granted all my life.

In return my wife and I both work harder to make Aaron aware of his environment and his place in it. It's always been about family. We all realize that we are in this for the long haul! I used to think that one day autism would just go away. No matter how hard we wish for things to be perfect, we have prepared ourselves to deal with reality. Every opportunity is significant and more importantly empowers our son's continued growth and development. The focus of our family is to seize every opportunity that can help our son move forward at a level he is both comfortable at maintaining and confident enough to maximize. With every changing aspect of his developmental and social experience, we are on a journey to realize a shared dream.

Aspirations are the window into a child's future; every child has aspiration in varying forms. I was recently at a baseball game for children with special needs. They all had various conditions, but a single common thread was very noticeable: they had an aspiration to do their best and enjoy the moment by competing, turning failure into success, and exceeding expectations. Aspirations are the stuff dreams are made of. I learned from this observation that aspiration does not have boundaries and is not tied to status and abilities.

It suddenly dawned on me that children with autism can also be exceptional in what they do. This way of thinking is always at the forefront as we help our son discover his strengths and talents and pursue his dream. The most powerful human influence is the idea of a dream.

Aaron has never expressed an interest in anything in particular. We kept looking for a hint from him. If it was there, we could not see it. So we exposed him to everything just to see where he would eventually land. I observed that when provided with an opportunity and some extra help, he is capable of accomplishing the unimaginable by unthinkably beating the odds against him.

I had so many of my own dreams all lined up and ready to go for my son. Fate has changed that. My gift to my son is to support his dream wherever it takes him. This is the only dream that counts.

I have had the privilege to network, socialize, and even share experiences with other fathers. I must confess that I am deeply moved by the fathers I've come into contact with. They display so much personal strength and character at a very stressful point in their own lives. I see the anguish and understand the frustration as we share war stories and discuss incidents at restaurants and other public places.

Amazingly, I have learned that there are other fathers who have managed to strike a balance between family, their personal well-being, and working twice has hard to make the best of a lifelong struggle with autism. On the other hand, I've met fathers who rather not discuss the matter; for them the pain and frustration is so evident that it becomes easier to just internalize the emotions, say nothing, and do the best they can without drawing attention to their child or to themselves.

Sometimes I feel so awkward and out of place when asking some fathers, "How are you doing today?" not knowing the reaction that will come from that. I am very aware of the fact that their dreams for their children have been dashed and expectations forever altered. As fathers we all share the same emotions and experiences to some degree. I understand the pain and frustration very well.

I will be the first father to agree that my dream for my child has been altered. However, the dream still lives, and I refuse to let it become dormant and die. As long as Aaron is willing to try, I am right there with him. When he gets tired and frustrated, I am in his corner to motivate and encourage him.

Encouragement, motivation, and mentoring are the secret to our son's success. I have personally chosen to take the active, not reactive role. Success is assured and becomes evident when autism is put into context. As a family we look at the future potential, not the current reality. With that in mind, anything is possible. My son is an example of this fact.

The first objective of this book is to share our son's story on his journey in pursuit of his ultimate dream, a dream hinged on the fact that he can reach his potential and be his best on his terms.

The second objective anchors on the hope that fathers can find inspiration and a fresh perspective from the pages of this book. We all have tipping points, no matter how strong we may appear to the outside world. Hey, we're only human! I personally will take all the good help and advice I can get if it provides my family with an advantage and advances my son's ability to succeed.

I am confident that the challenges and combined experience our family has endured speak volumes and will provide insight and inspiration to other families. I speak from a father's point of view as one who is "in the trenches," living and doing battle with autism every day.

Fathers I talk with express their appreciation for my personal insight about the challenges and opportunities encountered while raising a child with autism. Fathers find it rather refreshing to get the views of another father like me who is not afraid to share the positive aspects and potential of my son. Sharing my personal experience is a big hit with fathers, as it gives them some perspective and hope about how to overcome major personal challenges around the uncertain future of a child with autism, the frustration with family and friends passing insensitive comments and not understanding when you expect they would be more accommodating. I personally believe that this experience is another opportunity for me to show my humanity and caring for others. I want fathers raising a child with autism to know that ultimately their child like Aaron can exceed expectations. Reaching out to others is not just good for me but also serves as an example to my son. Bad things happen to good people. Our family makes every effort to turn autism into a positive experience. That is how we build a better world for each other and our kids with autism.

Most of the ideas we've come up with are unique in helping our son to accomplish a particular goal at a particular moment in time. The goals we set are realistic and achievable. Others are stretch goals just to test how much and how far he can really go. We have discovered that true potential and capabilities are dormant until put to the test. Aaron has achieved solid results because we started by thinking and acting unconventionally, in a way that was different than we used to.

Our family belief is that we have been blessed with a once-in-a-lifetime opportunity to work with a blank script. Not knowing where to start, we started with limited information and a dream that anything is possible even when the odds are stacked against us.

We believe that autism can be challenged to create positive outcomes. Creating this change has inspired and fueled hope that things will get better. This hope accentuates our belief that the possibilities encased in autism are limitless and ripe for discovery. When I see each small task Aaron accomplishes, each small change in behavior, we are all encouraged by the results.

Like so many parents, I have spent a vast amount of time researching volumes of information on the cause and symptoms of autism as well as asking questions about possible cures. A cure may not be available to help our son. However, we hope and pray a cure will eventually be discovered to help other children in times to come.

Autism has become a big adventure for us. We learn as we go to manage the unexpected situations in a positive way. Going through the development stages provides its own positive change and negative challenges. One positive change has been Aaron's ability to communicate openly with his immediate and extended family.

We have learned that as Aaron becomes more verbal he can inject his thoughts at any moment in any given situation without assessing the people that are around and the environment that he is in. At home he can say anything that comes to mind and sometimes it goes unnoticed. This communication experience has now extended to people outside our family circle which has created a challenge with the constant interrupting to get his point across during a conversation that is already in progress.

It is a little awkward and sometimes embarrassing in public to correct Aaron when there is a need to turn an incident into a learning moment. A lot of time is spent periodically redirecting him in the public setting where the interruption takes place. This works better for us and becomes a real time learning point for him. It is easier to be direct in a nice way rather than waiting till we get in the car and lose the teaching moment. Aaron is so keen to share information or just wants attention that I have to repeat the request for him to wait. This is very challenging, if it happens at school or in a public setting.

I used to be concerned about what other people might think if I corrected him for interrupting. The key is to redirect in a positive way. An example would be "can we discuss this in a minute" or "Just let me finish this conversation first and we can talk." There is always a mix of positive or negative experiences, depending on what takes place and how it is managed. We are seeing great progress as the interruptions are less frequent.

Positive reinforcements are by far the best and most effective tools to combat the many challenges to autism. We have seen the most encouraging results after applying what is basically a litany of "trial and error" experiments, intending to effectively manage the behavioral and social aspect of autism. It works every time. This discovery means that I can spend less time doing damage control and more time helping my son to enhance his strengths and unravel his potential so that he can be the best he can be. Our goal is for him to be prepared and to become more of an independent individual who will find success beyond his limitations, success on his terms, not ours. A child's character is his fate! The end depends upon the beginning.

One of the most precious lessons learned is that it is important to stay focused on a set of goals and maintain a positive attitude no matter what happens on a daily basis. This mindset defines how this journey will commence, continue, and end. We have made a conscious choice to help our son manage autism to the best of his ability. As a father I continue to give it my full attention! The results have been astoundingly positive and much more rewarding than I expected as the years go by. I reflect with great pride on this journey and the progress we have made together as a family.

My most important lesson learned as a father is anchored in the understanding that I need to "enjoy the journey," not the destination. There are so many uncertainties about the final outcome. What happens in the middle of the journey is far more important than the final outcome. It's taken me a while to get it! Now that I'm onboard, I find it easier to make the required lifestyle adjustments based on the fact that autism is here to stay, albeit in a milder and more controlled form!

Finding ways to make this a memorable journey has opened a window of opportunity for our family. We do everything together. We golf, wash the car, vacuum the house, go grocery shopping, cut the lawn, and visit the less fortunate and the sick. This experience has opened a window for Aaron. Because of this, our family relationship has naturally morphed into a more inclusive environment that has given our son a sense of belonging, normalcy, and involvement.

Our challenges have become fewer over time. Believe me; it becomes easier each and every day that goes by. It's more enjoyable, less stressful, and more fun. Being very optimistic about the future for Aaron was necessary for us to turn the negative into a positive experience. It's all about attitude and context. Our positive attitude enabled our family to get over the hump of desperation and helplessness to one of empowerment and engagement.

We've learned never to become complacent and relaxed. Time is of the essence, and there is never enough of it, especially in the early years of diagnosed autism. We have purposed ourselves to daily find new ways of putting a positive spin on every challenge, especially when the pressures and frustrations are all consuming and seemingly insurmountable. A positive attitude filled with golden-gem reminders that tomorrow will be better than today so often softens the fatigue and emotional and physical stress.

I always want to encourage fathers that I run into at various therapy sessions or at Special Olympics to never give up. It's so easy to feel sorry for ourselves to the point where we think that we are all alone and no one understands. This is one of the reasons why I've chosen to share the details of my experience: to help fathers understand that autism is not an end-all situation. It can and will get better. I'm an optimist, that's why I hang in there, try harder, and have never considered bailing out. I want to do the best I can for my child, even if it means trying harder when I feel drained physically and emotionally.

Sometimes, I get to the point where I have to convince myself that it's OK to be frustrated; then I can get over the frustration and move forward. It's really important to take some time out with each other as parents to recharge and energize. My recommendation for parents and caregivers would be to find an organization which provides "respite care." Respite care provides a safe and inclusive environment, which engages the clients and includes them in social events that are engaging.

There are a lot of church organizations that provide this service for free or at most a nominal fee. Searching on the internet under respite care will direct you to some good resources in your local and surrounding communities. Another option is to ask parents in your network about respite care. This time away from the routine of taking care of our son allows me and my wife to get away for a couple of hours. A little time away is all we need to recharge.

Going out for a quiet dinner or a long drive out prevents us from getting sucked into the daily grind; it is very important to break free a little bit and look for an opportunity, any reason to do stuff, change focus, and celebrate together. I asked Aaron where he would like to go for a special vacation, he said France. We planned the entire venture together. This is just one example on how to change the focus. It's an important part of the journey to unwind and recharge. Remember, it's what happens in the middle of the journey that counts, not at the end. Enjoy every moment; make it count for something memorable.Every learning aspect and social experience provides another opportunity for our children to expand, grow, and thrive against all the odds.

My son Aaron embraces a progressively independent lifestyle that functions around his restrictions and limitations resulting from the autism condition. Instinctively, every day he emerges with a new determination to outperform or outgrow many of his autistic traits because of our consistent and repetitive coaching on the importance of self-development and pursuing aspiration goals that are important to him. Today he is capable of making lasting and meaningful friendships. Tomorrow, he can thrive in his environment and live a quality of life that is second to none!

I can confidently say from my own experience that unwrapping my son's unique capabilities, which were shrouded under varying degrees of behavioral and learning challenges including development delays, has become much easier than I ever thought possible. He now emerges from the shadows of autism and the multiple development gaps to be the best he can be.

An achievement like this is fully realized as a result of

the repetitive daily process of continuous improvement. This is the concept of *Autism: Turning On the Light.*

This book is an inspiring way for me to share my experiences with fathers of children with autism. Sharing insight and hope about the great potential our kids are endowed with and the future possibilities of what our children can become is definitely worth putting pen to paper about. In the world of autism, parents need all the help and support we can get.

A psychologist who evaluated my son shared with me that in a lot of patients he sees, he can immediately tell that the lights are out and there is "nobody home." That was a very profound statement that had me thinking, *if the lights are out, what does it take to turn the lights on?*

I remember occasionally walking down the long, dark office corridor at my place of work and having to turn on a sequence of lights to illuminate the entire hallway before most of the office staff arrived in the morning. Raising a child with autism, I know that the lights were not on in many aspects of my son's cognitive thinking, behavior traits, and abilities.

It is conceivable that autism and its disabling tendencies can be drastically reduced to mild behaviors that are either mildly pronounced or not so readily noticeable. There is so much social awareness around autism. Combined with available and emerging resources, this growing social awareness will eventually help children like Aaron to successfully transition through the various stages of their lives, while making it so much easier to mix and blend into the social fabric of their environment.

Autism is very unpredictable when looking ahead into the future. It is rather difficult to determine which of those autistic challenges and tendencies will stick for the rest of his life or gradually disappear over time. But it is pretty clear to me as I compare and contrast my son Aaron's transition from full-blown autism to a milder side of the disorder that the impact of this change is making a profound difference in many aspects of his life, and creates a strong foundation for a bright and promising future ahead of him. Autism has brought along with it layers of expressive, behavioral, and emotional limitations, adding more complexity to the challenges Aaron has had to live with and overcome for many years. But real change is possible and inevitable because corrective action can be taken now!

CHAPTER 1:

A DAY IN THE LIFE

It's Monday. The school bus should be arriving at 6:30 a.m., and school starts at 7:30, but a typical school day routine for my son starts at 4:00 a.m. It is difficult for Aaron to wake up on time every morning and get prepared for school. He tries very hard to get me to help him with this preparation so that he is not late for the bus. It was important for Aaron to get himself prepared on time on his own. The bus would sometimes wait while he was rushing to finish his routine. I and my wife decided to get an alarm clock for his bedroom. I set the time, and he turns the alarm clock on at night and off in the morning. Next, we put a timer in the bathroom and set it for thirty minutes.

The next morning, the alarm goes off at 4:00 a.m.; Aaron turns it off and goes back to sleep. Then the timer goes off in the bathroom and he ignores it. This becomes a four-month project requiring constant reinforcement of the need to manage time. Ultimately we are able to cut bathroom time by fifteen minutes and decrease wake-up time by thirty. So, now he gets up at 4:30 every morning.

Getting through the shower, teeth, and dressing routine takes on average one hour. While he gets himself ready, the morning educational programs play on the TV; he can hear it down the hallway and through his bathroom floor. The programs run for approximately thirty minutes, and he normally goes through two of them before he gets downstairs for breakfast. Fruit and yogurt is prepared and on the table until Aaron comes down to independently finish making his cereal and waffles.

Access to early learning experiences and being exposed to math, reading, science, and literature through public television has really enabled our son in so many ways. The programming they offer has been a great supplement to the existing program he's on at school like the edmark reading program. Aaron practically learned advance language and reading skills by watching public television. Once we got past the age factor of the programs we found them to be an excellent tool.

Aaron repeatedly watches early education programming like Word World to help with basic word building concepts. Sesame Street helps with words, shapes, numbers and communication. Super Why helps with developing his ability to ask who, what, when, where and why questions. His programming viewing also includes Sid the Science kid, which helps him develop relationships and learning experiences with peers and friends on subjects of Science and Math, and Super Why which basically identifies more appropriate ways to ask questions and develop constructive thinking patterns. He has now excelled in these basic key learning areas that he struggled with at school. This list of public television children's early learning programming is a daily routine that sets the tone for his day and provides structure and content consistency to enable his learning and development experience.

We have approximately thirty minutes left which is just enough time to go over schoolwork. Carving out extra time in the morning to provide the extra help is what I call the "home-style head-start program." This morning regiment has helped tremendously to propel Aaron's development and speed up the learning process for him over time. I am now the uncertified "full-time" substitute teacher! It's all good and very rewarding.

With all the rushing around, we are bound to forget something. The bus arrives earlier than expected. Aaron is off to school and I head for work.

Midday my wife calls; she just got a call from the schoolteacher. Aaron is not focused, very hyperactive during the morning session, and not following directions. *Did you give him his medication? I think so! Maybe I didn't. OOPS!* Another important lesson learned: got to have a very close relationship with the teacher who will communicate behavior that is outside the norm on any given day.

I have to come up with a scheme that will prevent this from happening again. It helps to be proactive on issues rather than being reactive.

Our next goal is to go through the learning process associated with taking Aaron's medication at a certain time every morning without fail so that he can perform better throughout the school day. We both need to put in extra effort to remind each other so we will never forget again. We decide to place the medication in a visible place as a reminder to both of us. This goes well until there is another call from the school.

The next solution we come up with is to use a container with days of the week, something like a pillbox. In this we accomplish two tasks: learning the days of the week, and independently taking the medication daily. So, if Tuesday's medication is still in the container before breakfast is done, there's our reminder not to forget, as we continue rushing through the morning to complete Aaron's subject review before the school bus arrives.

Because Aaron could not self medicate during the day at school we had to give him a series of one time released tablets which works throughout the entire day. Timing when the medicine is dispensed in the morning was difficult to estimate. Getting the medicine too early or late would impact his focused during the day. This became another frustration point encountered in the beginning stages of creating a routine that works. We had to work closely with the teacher to provide us with feedback on his performance through a journal that would come home every day. We went through a series of extreme behaviors until we got it right. Finally, we found a time which works successfully, and we have stuck with it ever since.

My lesson learned in this instance is that it is challenging to be consistent and get it right the first time. I need to always collaborate with teachers to get better results. The way forward is to find a creative solution that works. Developing a method that is consistent and drives toward reinforcement of the goal is the goal! Being consistent and reinforcing the values that I feel are important for my child, such as time management and taking responsibility, helps to take some of the pressure off me.

Our success story is based on the ability to create basic goals and carve out as much time as possible on a daily basis to manage towards those goals. If we don't succeed today, we try again tomorrow with a different approach. Some days are just more challenging for Aaron and I as we work through different aspects of his basic learning goals. We measure success based on what is effectively managed at home; this automatically translates back to the time spent at school and his ability to stay on task and complete his core set of learning modules during a given day. We are not working for perfection; we are working on continuous improvement.

CHAPTER 2:

REFLECTIONS

My greatest joy is the birth of my son Aaron. Everything was perfect. My wife and I were ready to go and start a new chapter of our lives! We made all the necessary plans for Aaron to have a well-balanced, successful, and fulfilling life. We set aside resources for the best of everything. This was supposed to be an easy journey with a couple of unexpected hurdles and bumps in the road.

As Aaron started growing, we noticed certain traits and behaviors that seemed odd. We became increasingly concerned about them. He enjoyed playing by himself a lot. My initial reaction was that he was demonstrating a strong sign of independence and confidence at a very young age a type of self-starter attitude, if you know what I mean.

Then it turned to self-stimulation and an obsession with string and turning wheels. He had delays in walking.

After going through a battery of tests and being referred to a couple of specialists, we were informed that Aaron was autistic with the addition of ADHD. My greatest pride turned into unthinkable tragedy.

I thought that the specialist had gotten the diagnosis wrong. I respect doctors for their training and experience, but as far as I was concerned, this time they'd gotten it wrong. How could they say with 100 percent surety that Aaron had autism and ADHD? I had no intention of going back to that doctor. We need a second and, if I was not satisfied a third opinion. I was hoping for someone, anyone to tell me what I wanted to hear.

I thought hard and long on whether there was any history of autism in my own or my wife's family. It was impossible to accept any of this. But the more specialists we saw, the more it was apparent that there were not wide variations to this diagnosis.

There was a time when I believed that even if what the doctors diagnosed was true, Aaron would grow out of it. Together as a family we would beat this. We could not find a doctor to collaborate or reaffirm these beliefs. So I gave up on the specialists and convinced my wife that Aaron would grow out of it, given time.

How could this happen? What went wrong? What could we have done differently? I had all these questions and no answers. All I know was that what we considered as our dream had changed forever.

I was in the dumps and needed to get out from under this cloud that was engulfing me very fast.

This announcement affected how I interacted with family, friends, and associates. I felt boxed in, and there was no way out. Everywhere I turned there was uncertainty and disappointment at the onset. The hardest challenge was not that our son was diagnosed on the autism spectrum but for me to understand what happened, get comfortable with it, and move on.

The solution was going to be difficult but straightforward: be sensitive but be a strong role model as well as a dad.

Going through the stages and getting comfortable with autism has been one of my most difficult challenges. Embracing autism is not an easy task. It is not unusual that men find it easier to walk away than to have to deal with such a drastic change emotionally, financially, physically, and mentally.

The first stage was trying to have somewhat of a normal life through this change in events, like going to a restaurant as a family. We would get those stares and sometime sly comments or the unwelcome body language and gestures from people who just were not walking in our shoes. Parents measured their kids to mine and became uncomfortable being around us. They did not say one word, but actions do speak louder than words. I was always reacting to that behavior, and then I realized it was not intentional. It did make life awkward and uncomfortable for me as a parent. As for our son, he could not have cared less!

That's when it dawned on me: Why worry about the things I cannot change? Just focus on changing the things I can. That was a big attitude adjustment for me as a parent of a child with autism. We started to do things differently, including getting seats in a secluded area at restaurants. This helped to contain the behaviors and allowed us to enjoy a meal without the public scrutiny.

Then there were other public places, like the park or the supermarket. All this was a learning experience. I found that I was thinking differently to cope with this condition that affects our son.

When Aaron was to start pre-kindergarten, the teacher asked us to go and visit Aaron's new school and speak to his teacher. We were informed that he needed to go into a special class because of a learning deficit, which was discussed among the teachers without informing us. We were very surprised by the choice they suggested for our son. We felt betrayed by the school system. They did not fully disclose what we were being asked to commit our son to.

We found it difficult to trust that school with our child, after a decision to move him to a school setting that was not going to challenge him to be his best. We were very concerned that there was no teacher parent consultation, and no other options were on the table. It was like the school was telling us to take it or leave it! The solution was to move our family to another school district that would not make us feel like we were being forced into a box of unpleasant circumstances which could limit our son's options to communicate in a class of non-verbal children. This is counterproductive for our son and his future.

Lesson learned: no matter what I am being told or advised on about Aaron, I am always thinking about how well Aaron will transition into the community, work and having a good quality of life which is the ultimate goal for Aaron.

We explained in detail to the new school teacher our experience at the school district we just left. How the school system limited our choices for Aaron to be in a challenging environment that he could grow and develop his capabilities. The teacher at the new school understood what we were doing. We were only trying to find the best school options which would cater to Aarons special needs. We were afraid of making bad choices for our son at the beginning cycle of his school life, which we would have to live with for the rest of our lives. We knew that there is a better school option for Aaron and we were prepared to find it.

The teachers at the new school system helped me and my wife tremendously. They explained Aaron's diagnosis as an umbrella. Under the umbrella there are many spectrums of autism, mild to severe. The teachers explained that depending on treatment and his ability to adopt change, he could float from severe to mild autism over time. I needed some reassurance that everything was not as bad as the other school had made me to believe. We were certain that we made the right choice by moving to this new school system. Aaron loved the teachers, who are very interactive and helpful. He was able to mix with mainstream classes for some subjects or activities like art and PE which is our aspiration goal for Aaron.

CHAPTER 3:

Autism Unwrapped

Navigating autism is an education and a tremendous learning experience. There is no rulebook or standard operating procedure for us to follow. Most of what my wife and I know now about autism, we have learned as a family through independent study and research on numerous occasions or just by making some mistakes along the way. Many times I had no other choice but to burn the midnight oil just trying to make sense of what information was useful to help us overcome a problem with Aaron's behavior which was getting in the way of his development. Most times it was like shooting in the dark just hoping for some new, helpful discovery.

It's now been seven years reading up on the subject of autism. Along the way it became apparent to me that there is a tremendous amount of focus on the science and cause of autism as defined by experts, doctors, researchers, educators, and advocates for autism awareness.

However, the more research I pursued, the more I realized I was still unclear about the practical next steps I should be taking. I kept thinking that something was missing! Resources that could help me connect and take cues from another father who had already traveled this road were not readily available. There is certainly a lot of very good information, but it was all abstract on a personal level.

In order to get access to this more personal, practical information, I turned to parent-to-parent and other focus group meetings for solid help and advice.

During many of these meetings I was the only male attending, which surprised me until I realized that like me every father is so busy with other matters.

However, I was still having a hard time getting my mind around this absence. I started to have this undying concern regarding how other fathers of these children were making it. What were their personal experiences, challenges, frustrations, and concerns? How difficult were they finding it to communicate with family, friends, and coworkers about the stress, anxiety, and helplessness they experienced? I could not help but wonder!

A father shared how he would erase and photo-copy all the information from his child's school work which kept coming back home incomplete. This father set time aside so that his child could do the same problems at home. Whatever was wrong he would focus on that specific piece of information until his child got the concept by way of repetition. It is a time-consuming effort. A lot of erasers were used to accomplish this task.

The lesson from this is coming up with creative out-of-the-box ideas to help our children advance and succeed over obstacles. Aaron and your child can overcome their trial and tribulations; they can do-it, with guidance and support. It is evident that fathers of children on the autism spectrum have a wealth of experience and valuable insight to share with other fathers having similar experiences all over the world.

Fathers continue to suffer in silence and are very quiet in a world dominated by bias, cynicism, insensitivity and lack of concern when the topic of a child with special needs comes up and the "Retard" word is used very loosely in casual conversations. Fathers of children with autism can change this perception by demonstrating the hard work and effort our children put into overcoming obstacles to become productive and well adjusted citizens in their communities.

Just listening to the mothers was a tremendous learning experience. I picked up more information from them than any research or academic material could ever provide. The information they shared was practical, insightful, and honest. I gained enough confidence and understanding that it became much easier to speak the language of autism with parents who are living and coping with autism its challenges, accomplishments, and dreams. Like Aaron, dreams embraced by children living with autism are being realized one dream at a time. I learned that it's the little things that really matter along the journey.

Before I got involved in the litany of meetings and focus groups for autism, my wife would download for me whatever she had picked up or learned along the way. I was not always tuned in because I was so mentally drained, even though what she shared with me was good. Sometimes it just takes a little longer to absorb and take in what is being explained. I learned that there is no shame in coming back and saying, "Can you explain that again?" Many times it was difficult for me to follow through on ideas and sound advice immediately.

It really comes down to putting in the effort to stay focused and listen to the important information my wife is trying to share, and filter out my personal distractions. It is so much easier just to carve out the time to actually be there and be present in mind and body.

My personal learning, experience, and exposure from ongoing engagement with various parent network groups have changed my entire approach and thinking about how I can do things differently to take some of the load of my wife. Some of the changes I made included taking time off work to do the Doctor or therapy visits, and parent teacher sessions at school. Taking on those early morning therapy appointments that were not always convenient helped my wife immensely. It's all about doing more with a limited amount of available time. I went from being unsure about what I knew to fully embracing every opportunity to help my son, my wife and myself with much zeal and new enthusiasm.

I genuinely started to feel that my family was not alone in this situation. This was very comforting! I picked up a wealth of knowledge from the practical support groups with respect to the pitfalls of not doing enough to fully support and genuinely be there for my special needs child, and most of all for my wife. My eyes were opened by the mothers expressing their feelings about feeling neglected. I became very sensitive and considerate about what to do and what not to do to prevent my family from feeling neglected because of the stress of raising a child with autism. A lot of the information shared was personal, and most parents were OK about sharing this because we were all on the same path with more or less the same goals and objectives. The spotlight was focused on our children with autism.

I have since been presented with many opportunities to share my experience with fathers in therapists' and doctors' office, and even at ball games.

The feedback I sometimes get is very direct. Understandably, there are a lot of emotions mixed with the view that "everybody has their own problems" so why make the world any worse by sharing them? On the surface this is true; however, fathers can find strength, inspiration, and encouragement to continue by networking with like-minded parents who have very similar experiences, challenges, and desired outcomes. When experiences are shared in an honest, open, and respectful manner, I have seen the relief on many fathers' faces as their eyes light up. Many times it's pretty obvious that their reaction indicates "I just learned something new!"

Finding assurances to make fathers feel good about the future of their children on the autism spectrum can sometimes be just a phone call away as we do a better job of connecting and supporting each other. Occasionally, fathers struggle with the barriers which their child has to endure due in part to the lack of funding in many areas, from good research to basic social services. Organizing our effort to share information and cheer for our children is a big win for fathers. In the quest to find a little spot of validation I have found that by creating a supportive environment which will help Aaron to succeed we have all won.

Many fathers for good reasons still believe that they are alone in this fight. There are so many unresolved situations that families with special needs come up against, and when they are put together it becomes so easy to get hung up on the things we cannot influence and lose sight of the things we can. This becomes the perfect environment for discouragement and frustration. It all boils down to being able to build a network and community around the family with like-minded parents, friends, and children to help build the support we all are desperate for in those times of personal need. We can all help, support, and educate each other as a community on this journey striving for better outcomes for our children. That is the bottom line of all our efforts!

The most valuable piece of information that I can share with fathers of children with special needs is the importance of interacting and constantly surrounding themselves with people who have good information which has been personally tested and is capable of being put into immediate action. Fathers can be very influential and more effective when ideas are bounced of other fathers. My thing is "tell me what works and I'll do it." It's not about what I think but about what I really know!

Sound advice and good information is all I have to offer from the pages of this book. I am so grateful for the various support groups, teacher/mentors, and other parents who have helped me overcome my narrow view about autism. These parents have helped me to get to a place where I feel more confident about moving forward, armed with solid, actionable information and insight, and gaining experience along the way. This is a good place to be. Every opportunity I get, I use this information to help and inspire other fathers of children with autism who are trying to do their best by stepping up to the plate for their loved ones. I am a father of a child with autism and I am empowered!

CHAPTER 4:

ONCE I WAS BLIND

One night I was driving down a country road with the lights at full brightness, illuminating everything in my path and making it easy to see what lay ahead. I turned the lights off for a moment, and in an instant I couldn't see anything, much less determine if I was still on the road. And so it is when dealing with autism. We are creating and charting a path through the darkness for our children which is very clear to all of us.

The path we have created to help Aaron overcome autism requires a lot of discipline and often becomes very demanding on our son. The routine is constant but we often mix up the schedule so it becomes interesting and easier for him to accept. The demanding schedule mixed with some flexibility to play and be a child gets better results. We are now seeing some encouraging and progressive signs of improvement in his ability to learn, retain and rehearse information. This is a light of hope for us and we believe that better days are ahead for him. I and my wife have chosen to do everything in our power using all the resources at our disposal to support Aaron and his development beyond Autism. I have committed myself to go above and beyond the basic therapy sessions to challenge autism head-on for my child.

First it was important to manage my time better. Second it was just so hard to challenge myself to do things differently. I had a lot of great ideas about how to get the best possible outcome for my son. However, my enthusiasm was constantly interrupted by work and other responsibilities. There was never enough time in the day to take action on all the good plans. Eventually, I just got tired of making excuses. My motivation started when I realized that fathers can be very influential. I discovered there is definitely a difference between being enthusiastic about the future and finding that motivation to help propel me and my child forward into a future that is bright, rewarding, fulfilling, and safe.

A lot of my focus is placed on those behavioral and developmental techniques that improve my son's ability to have lifelong relationships and a stronger bonding experience between father and child.

Aaron's struggle to succeed and overcome the limitations autism has placed on him is truly inspiring. He has so much potential, which I couldn't see at first no matter how I tried. Aaron has helped me to turn my approach to autism around in a positive way by first overcoming my doubts and personal feelings about what autism has done to our family.

Fathers, don't leave it up to the mothers! Get involved. I've become so engaged now that a lot of business travel which kept me from home for extended periods of time had to be kept to a minimum. The increasing social activities with friends and colleagues which consumed a major part of my available time had to take second place to spending more time with my son. I started to spend more time at school meetings and special needs events. I learned a lot about what it takes to truly be engaged with Aaron. The experience was great. I felt that I was truly making a difference. This is a real empowering experience for me. Investing the time and effort to support his lifelong development helps me to be part of the solution. I finally realized that what I put in is what we get out! It feels good to see the progress from each milestone change as the lights of learning, understanding, communicating, following directions, appropriate behavior management, which were dim as a result of autism come on one by one.

Those innate capabilities that come naturally to most of us without much consideration, like communication, are for the most part lacking in children with autism. It was much easier for me to say yes to everything my son was trying to communicate even when it was not clear to me. My challenge was to develop enough patience to restate the question and then wait for his response. We repeated this exercise over a period of time. Now if I incorrectly repeat something he said he will correct me if I am wrong. My communication style with Aaron improved because I took the time to listen. Aaron has taught me that I can be very influential to help him communicate better and clearer with everyone he comes in contact with because now he is not afraid to politely say "I think you misunderstood."

Grooming a child with autism to succeed and develop a well-rounded set of core values at his or her own pace requires a lot of self-sacrifice and constant recitation of concepts and ideas between parent and child. This value system helps to set the foundation for an independent and self-sufficient future.

But many times parents are so busy doing stuff that they never take the time to acknowledge the fact that what they are accomplishing is monumental and truly a labor of love. We all get tired and frustrated. However, there is an end goal in mind. One day with great pride we will look back and reflect on how much everything was worth it. I know I will!

The dream we embrace for Aaron is anchored on continuous improvement. Finding different ways to minimize the autistic behaviors he displays is an enormous challenge. He is totally dependent on our ability to groom, support, coach, and be his mentor. Grooming, mentoring, and coaching have become the brick-and-mortar elements that have built a foundation from which every one of his development milestones have ascended.

Aaron exceeded our expectations two years after

we were told by a lot of professionals that he would not be able to do a lot of basic things a regular child would normally do! For a moment we were convinced that autism was this monumental task that we were not equipped for or capable of dealing with. Moreover, in the beginning we didn't know how to influence meaningful change for our son.

With the help of God and our families, and their love, support, and commitment, Aaron has turned the corner and continues to improve every day. Every day is an unexpected surprise. Change has come in unexpected forms. On the first day visiting a two day camp for children with special needs we noticed as parents were coming up and dropping their kids off, Aaron asked a young girl in the wheel chair if he could push her inside. This was unexpected and very thoughtful. Another lady asked him if she could hug him and he gave her a hug with the shoulder side of his body. This is unusual for children with autism to extend a hand to help someone else in need and to allow anyone to embrace them willingly. The willingness to give respect and receive it can only help his social development.

This is just another example of our efforts to engage Aaron in out-of-the-box creative thinking through continuous improvement and redirection. Is it easy? No! But the dream continues for our son. With every passing moment the impossible is becoming very possible. It has been a long, painful, and joy-filled journey. I realize how much "I was once blind to the upside potential of autism" but now I see!

CHAPTER 5:

LET'S FIX IT

This chapter is about fostering Aaron's growth and trying different approaches without pushing to unattainable boundaries he cannot possibly reach. There is never any harm to push Aaron beyond his immediate capabilities, to interact with mainstream children. Boys and Girls Club of America proved that Aaron can adapt over time to improve the way he communicates with others. One of the biggest surprises is that he knows everyone at the club by first name.

This experiment to fix his unsocial behavior worked. We took a big risk by allowing Aaron to attend the local Boys and Girls Club. The club leaders are very accommodating to Aaron and his special needs. The club has one hundred and fifty to two hundred kids coming through that center on a daily basis. We were afraid he would be lost and lonely if the kids ignored him because of his disability. Fortunately Aaron made new friends and was able to build a good relationship with the main stream kids at the club. Another plus was his special needs friends from school also attending the club.

I tried so many different ways to fix autism, with a one-size-fits-all approach including enrolling Aaron to participate in gymnastics, soccer, baseball and mainstream activities at school. It doesn't work very well with autistic children. Creating other opportunities for him to spend more time around mainstream kids helped his adjustment to the immediate social setting at social gatherings and school. Aaron gravitated to the kids who wanted to be his friend. To those kids his condition is not an issue. This meant that his friends were younger. His peers made him feel uncomfortable by ignoring him more often than not. It is devastating to watch how hard Aaron tries to connect with his peers. The maturity levels are not the same.

As painful as it seemed this exercise helped to strengthen his confidence as well as his understanding that everyone is not his friend, which is a major challenge we tried so hard to fix. To avoid his peers there have been instances when all he wanted was to play with the latest gadgets and toys. He would entertain himself with the toys not to socialize. I wanted so desperately to give those toys away. I constantly try very hard to help Aaron beat the unsocial behaviors.

My natural reaction when something is not working right is to immediately jump into the problem and "fix it!" Breaking stuff apart only just to fix it again is my way of keeping touch with my creative side. More times than not I am successful, but there have been other times when I really failed miserably. Sometimes I failed to the point of giving up.

After Aaron was diagnosed with autism, I was devastated, heartbroken, and disappointed all at the same time. It took me two years to get myself untangled from all the mixed emotions and personal feelings that kept clouding my thinking. I kept myself busy at work and doing other things to change my focus. Aaron was now two years older and his autistic tendencies did not change. I decided that enough is enough. "We are going to overcome autism if it's the last thing I have to do." To be honest I just needed some space to adjust. Time really changed my way of thinking. I transitioned from a state of confusion to believing that I could "fix" autism. I was totally fixated on this idea; it became my new purpose and passion in life. This was my way to make it right for my son. Apparently, I was just making it right for me.

Despite my enthusiasm and good intentions, I ended up compounding an already unique and complicated situation. Approaching my son's condition like one of my pet projects was not the best solution. Ironically, the more I struggled to make my son normal I convinced myself that I could fix this condition by putting in a little more extra time and effort into it.

Change was not happening too quickly. I was disappointed and refused to think out of the box for another solution. My approach needed a good re-think. Lesson learned: I need to be more flexible and creative in my thinking without rigidity.

For a moment I started comparing my child to other children on the autism spectrum to find some measure of comfort. I started thinking that it was not all that bad. Looking at the big picture; it could have been much worse. Maybe, I was trying so hard, too hard to fix the problem.

I was frustrated and began to lose perspective and sight of the real goal: to help my son be the best he can be. Eventually I forced myself to start thinking outside the box. That's when new ideas started to open up other possibilities and opportunities, which ultimately have become part of Aaron's progressive development plan in a more nurturing environment. Nurturing is based on my personal involvement without the pressure of pushing me and my son to get quick results no matter the cost. It became apparent that the fix-it idea was narrow and only focused on the here and now without really addressing the need for a longer-term solution.

I soon realized that quick fixes, no matter how well intended, do not create the path to long-term solutions. A long-term plan is the best and only way to obtain lasting and productive outcomes in the fight against autism. Bottom line, I had to figure out a way to develop Aaron's unique abilities without the desperate pushing and pulling to get results. Quick fixes which appealed to me included the newest magic pills that would improve the effects of autism over a two year period. When that did not work I turned to the latest therapies. This was an option I was willing to pursue because it seemed to offer an immediate solution for a desperate parent, willing to take a chance with something, anything that could remotely change and improve Aaron's situation.

Still not willing to give up my "can do attitude," I turned to another idea around sleep disorders to manage autism. If managed properly through a series of routine sleep patterns it was possible to reduce the effects of autism. This routine became hard to manage and harder to consistently enforce. Aaron would reject this option because he was not ready to sleep. This was all becoming an overwhelming exercise with very little results.

Learning from what does not work I realize that patience is also a necessary ingredient. A lot of patience is needed to help Aaron thrive in his environment so he will flourish at his own pace in his own time

I was becoming more willing to let go of my emotions and just do the best I can without trying to do the impossible.

As I have started to loosen up my son just wanted to do more even when it was beyond his ability. I have never met a kid who does not try their very best to make their parents proud of their accomplishments. Autistic children try harder to express this inner desire in their own way. My son has taught me that if he is doing his best I should work with that. Honestly, I only want the best for him. I feel that I have let him down if

I do anything less. One of the small areas we started to work on to fix some of the developmental and cognitive challenges was to reinforce a sense of pride in small accomplishments.

Telling the time accurately to the half hour or five minutes, making his bed and other household chores is rewarded with thirty minutes on his favorite computer game. This is a confidence booster no matter what the levels of abilities are.

In his own way, my son tries to be confident in everything he does. Every day he gets better at completing a task after many tries, and that becomes the building block for the next phase. It's not an easy role to be in but "all things are possible to them that try." In his mind, Aaron knows that he can thrive and do well with a little extra help and coaching from Mom and Dad. Coaching is the connecting tissue that helps to bridge and develop all deficiencies.

This journey has been a continuous cycle of reassessing the situation to make sure that the path we're on makes sense over the long term. There is no right or wrong way; it's all about finding what works for your child. There have been periods of slow to little results, even after multiple periods of reinforcing behaviors and continuous repetition of tasks and expectations. In the back of my mind I am convinced that by being patient and consistent with my methods Aaron's condition will change over the long-term. I am learning every day to get comfortable with autism being our new normal, be at peace with it and never stop pushing for continuous improvement. I do not have all the answers, but I will try to find them.

My real goal has always been to find a solution which works best for Aaron. Believe me, there is no "secret formula to autism. "The solution to autism has to be as unique as the child.

I am very proud of Aaron. He tries harder than I ever could or would if I were in his shoes. I see his willingness to continuously improve himself. He does not get frustrated as he tries and tries again until he gets his task right. I have no idea what he's going through to make sense of it all. Despite my eagerness to help, I find myself helpless up to a point. All he needs is time to fix the pieces and connect the dots in his own way, so that it makes sense and enables him to build greater self-confidence.

Time and the consistent attention to small details, including some extra coaching from me as his father, is prompting him to adopt his own rhythm and style of learning and retaining information. My coaching methods are very simple. Teach, by example. If he says a word out of context we go through the steps to correct it. Training, dedicating an appropriate amount of time and being practical are my coaching methods used to support and guide Aaron.

I use the coaching approach very regular and consistently to give Aaron more opportunity to take the initiative. I used to read an entire book to Aaron.

He now reads the same book with minor prompting on words which are still challenging for him. I continued the same process for math and all other learning steps. Essentially I stopped doing everything for him. Coaching has been a very strong element to manage and retrain Aaron's thinking, communication, and behaviors.

I discovered that coaching Aaron encourages respect, clarity in his method of communication, socialization, confidence, and the ability for him to complete tasks and functions willingly and independently. These abilities have been a major challenge for our son. Coaching has become the bridge for him to transition from major developmental delays to achieving success against his learning goals. Fathers can be very influential when it comes to coaching. Fathers do it naturally because of the competitive sports element.

Over many years Aaron has accepted and acted on a lot of the coaching efforts that my wife and I have shared with him. Sometimes there is resistance that we have to deal with creatively. His rejection of the coaching effort is just another invitation to take a different approach to the same challenge. I have been through many bouts of rejection only to come out with a workable-solution. Sometimes the whole process feels like I am in a negotiation. If I don't succeed the first time, I try another approach, hoping to yield better results.

The real learning experience and take away from this for me is the importance of being a consistent mentor and coach with a willingness and persistence to offer guidance and support when it is appropriate. Sometimes as a father I feel pity clouds my judgment when dealing with Aaron. Sometimes I am unwilling to push him to do more. He does not need pity; he needs my love and devotion which can be very reassuring. Our goals are lofty but very flexible to a point.

Has coaching worked for Aaron? Oh yes, it has! Ask his pastor, teacher, therapist, doctor, and they will all say the same thing.

My frustration and anxiety levels have been reduced to the point where it is easier for me and Aaron to work together more harmoniously as a team. There is also less conflict. It all boils down to a plan and consistent follow-through of the plan. The effort required to help my son was more than I was capable of giving due to the many commitments competing for my time. I was slowly getting to a point where I was tired to do anything extra. After a while I started to make adjustments on where my time is focused. One example was to go to bed early and get up early. Being a morning person, I was at my most productive. Aaron and I completed a tremendous amount of work. So even when I came home late we were still in good shape.

I was told a story about a parent with an autistic child who would exhibit very unsocial behaviors. One day the father decided to lie down with him during one of these incidents. The child immediately calmed down, and there was a sense of relationship established. What just happened? The father entered his child's space, the space that was sacred. The child soon realized that his dad was his friend, and responded playfully. This was the beginning of the bonding process.

I have gained greater success from being aware of my son's need for bonding and the timing required for me to get in touch with him and his specific needs. I now know when to give him space and when to reengage. It's all art and has nothing to do with science. Sometimes I have had to take Aaron out on a father and son field trip for ice-cream, have some fun and a good chat. This is just another conscious effort to help fix certain behaviors that I can help to influence. I understand Aaron's needs better and what he is dealing with as he struggles to share his thoughts and frustrations. He understands what I am dealing with in order to help him as much as I can. It does not have to be always verbal communication, only a common understanding between both of us.

No matter what goes down, we are buddies as well as father and son. Aaron tries very hard to communicate his feelings more often because he wants to. Whenever he needs me I am ready to talk. This is much better than pushing communication on him because I want him to get better at speaking and communicating. If he wants to talk about computer games which I am not the expert on, we talk about that. I prefer that he talk to me on anything rather than ignore me. I look forward to following his lead for us to play basketball, ride the bike or do regular father and son activities. Gone are those days when I would do all the talking with very little response from him.

Every day there is a tremendous need to keep the lines of communication open, or else Aaron goes back into his own world and shuts us out. So I do the talking and he does the listening. Now he does the talking and I try to say "please keep quiet!"

Putting it in context I am grateful that we have come to this point in his development that he wants to freely and openly communicate. In the beginning it seemed like Aaron would never open up at all. For me, this is progress. I can confidently say that to get the maximum progress out of a child with autism, there always has to be an understanding moving in both directions. It's not always about me pushing my agenda which can be counterproductive if not managed well. Aaron loves music and computer games, so we use that as a medium to develop and build our communication skills with each other this will lead to other areas to inspire greater motivation as he attempts to take on more learning and development tasks. I feel the overwhelming responsibility and obligation to do whatever it takes to make this relationship work, as difficult as it may be at times.

So, it's no more a matter of trying to fix anything; it's about building the relationship. Growing up with a child on the autism spectrum has evolved into one of the most challenging yet rewarding experiences ever.

It's definitely extra work for our family, but I count my blessings.

I strongly believe that you have to be a special parent selected for this experience. This life journey offers the selected few an opportunity to embark on an unusual sequence of events that require patience, common sense, love, and some more patience to the nth degree!

Patience was never my sweet-spot. I am learning that it is important to dig deeper for better answers and solutions to improve Aaron's overall development. My son has inspired me to be the best dad for him. For every learning experience that was bad, there was another coming to make up for it. This is what inspires hope in our family. I was given another opportunity after many failures to rethink my strategy and develop a more hands-on approach, not using traditional methods of behavior modification that I was accustomed to using.

Reinforcing strengths and developing weaknesses is the fundamental and basic set of ground rules for our family and has become the premise for this book. When Aaron succeeds, we all succeed and celebrate. When we fail, we learn from the mistakes and move forward. This has become an extensive investment of time, but it is worth every moment.

There is light at the end of this tunnel. All it takes to get there is an open mind and a lot of invested extra time, sacrifice, and love. Our child is a special child with specific needs; in every respect this adds to his uniqueness.

This uniqueness becomes more evident and apparent through every milestone reached and successive accomplishments.

The experience alone for our family is a once-in-a-lifetime occurrence. We have been challenged beyond our individual abilities to think and act in ways not imagined. But collectively we are moving mountains.

CHAPTER 6:

ENJOY THE JOURNEY

Learning the value and experience of making every moment count is one of the fundamental principles our family has adopted. It's so easy to get carried away with the end goal and miss the finer moments that become lasting memories along the way. Four years went by so fast just trying to keep up with a busy schedule. This was a period when our time was absorbed with more commitments than we could manage. This way of life was just not sustainable, and the schedule was driving us crazy. Every moment we had available was spent trying to make and keep appointments, both locally and out of town. We were very concerned that missing an opportunity to give Aaron what he needed at any point in time would be devastating. Because of our actions and good intentions, we restricted our effort to really enjoy the beauty and splendor of family life.

We finally realized that the whole person needed to be attended to, not the part. This was an opportunity we were not willing to let pass us by. Today we still have a busy schedule; however, we have learned to enjoy the lighter moments and every experience that we encounter along the way. Communication is much better and more thoughtful. On the weekend we really do have a week's end to unwind and be a family. It has taken us years to get to this point.

Everything used to be so planned for us. We still have deadlines and time frames to manage, but we also slowed down and are taking it one day at a time. Everything is not a fire drill or mad rush for the door anymore. I and my wife made adjustments to our schedules and lifestyle. This has helped to keep the family together and in touch with each other. We took this approach because we wanted the end to be something we could all be proud of and reflect on without too many regrets.

Right now we are much more motivated than ever, because some of the burdens are not so heavy anymore. The continuous effort and hard work does not feel like it used to. Aaron has the opportunity to be a well-rounded person through the many life experiences that we are able to offer him as a result of our unplanned family events and trips all over the country. We continue to mentor and coach him like there is no autism or disability. We have mentored and coached him so that he is aware of his condition. However, the focus is "let's just be ourselves." It's very important for him to have a well-rounded personality and set of experiences; this is part of his long-term development plan and our personal aspiration for him.

I have my sights on "what the end of this journey is going to look like." Personally, it keeps me awake at night, because there is not a definite or predictable path that I can draw comfort from. I get very concerned about the future. This is at sometimes a source of stress that I try to work through. I believe in having a plan. It makes me feel that I am not missing important opportunities to advance my son in his learning and development.

We continue to set medium and short-term goals for our son and ourselves so that we are all in alignment. The short-term goals hinge on continuous improvement, and the medium-term goals focus on stretching. Mixed into our goals is also time set aside to have fun along the way. That's normal and helps to keep things real and engaging for our family. We decided a long time ago to expose our son to everything that would allow him to mature and develop, whether competing in sports, becoming learned and traveled, through education experiences, or helping him to understand and have a sense of culture and respect for others by helping the elderly neighbor take her groceries inside her house or drop by and say hi.

Has this worked for us? Oh, yes! The environment we've created provides a balance for Aaron to learn, grow, and have fun. The tradeoff is that we are breaking the routine of home, work and school which our son can predict and explain if asked. Being spontaneous is about when we go away for short weekends, jump on a bus to nowhere, and do things that are not planned. Aaron is challenged to communicate what he did, where he went and how long he stayed.

The outgoing lifestyle which my wife and I enjoy helps Aaron understand that he can break routine. Now he is not so resistant to going out and having new experiences. It's still not a perfect situation. Sometimes staying at home and going back to his routine means that we have to cancel events and trips. I can only do so much fixing. Autism is a very powerful influence. Aaron is different in his unique way and I respect his decision to not want to go out and be spontaneous like his mother and I. We respect each other for who we are and for what we bring to the "table of life."

Keeping a balance along the way gives Aaron a sense of purpose as he realizes what is expected of him. Every day we engage in activities that are inclusive for him so he feels he is a part of the family with a voice and a seat at the table.

Our family loves swimming. We had Aaron take swimming lessons for two years, and every time he would be denied an opportunity to advance to the next level because he was not quick enough to grasp basic concepts and instructions. So we decided to get a swimming pool. Aaron splashed around then learned to float; now he's doing the backstroke.

The lesson from this is always look for another

alternative to prove your child can do what everyone else says he or she cannot. Now we go to the local gym, and he swims the full length of an Olympic-size pool. When summer comes around, he's ready for the beach.

Aaron also likes gymnastics; however, he was never good enough to advance to the next level. So we allowed him to do karate. He was able to use some of the gymnastic training and soon after became a yellow belt. He is working towards the next belt.

Exposure to these two activities became the pathway for our son to extend his abilities. We ask him what he wants to do, and then we just go and do it! If we run into roadblocks, we get creative again. The lesson Aaron is learning from us is that nothing is impossible, no matter the ability or disability. Through these experiences we learn on the go while creating lasting memories. His therapists have commented that Aaron does not give up. Children live what they learn.

"Enjoying the journey, not the destination" is not a cliché for our family; it is the way we've chosen to help our son work hard on his cognitive and social development but have fun in the process. The sky is the limit. I've found it very counterproductive to only focus on the development and learning deficiencies. It is important to us that he embraces a 360-degree approach to his life from a cognitive, behavioral, social, and emotional perspective. It's important for him and us that he adjusts well into every day society. That is important to me and requires my full attention and support in addition to the support and exposure provided by his teachers and private therapists.

Allocating enough time to enjoy the lighter side of life beyond the to-do list and therapy sessions has proved to be a very successful, providing a balanced mixture that allows Aaron to be more focused on his various tasks and activities. A lot of his challenging behaviors have diminished or gone away. We noticed that he feels more understood and more confident, and believes that we are trying to make his life happy and successful. Success is hinged on creating memorable experiences that drive toward better outcomes.

We still do have the occasional awkward moments, which are a candid reminder that even though great progress has been made, it's not a perfect situation. It's all part of the journey and the learning experience. We take the good with the indifferent and make it a learning moment to be developed and celebrated when success is achieved.

It has taken a while for us to get to this point where a strong sign of confidence is maturing in Aaron as a direct result of exposure to everyday experiences. A lot of milestones and goals have been accomplished as a result of these opportunities. There have been a lot of activities in which he was unable to participate at school. He's been disappointed by this one time too many because of his condition, so we bridged the gap at home.

Today, he is mixing with the general population in

a number of different social settings. Adapting to his new social settings can be challenging, even sometimes demanding, but that's OK, as Aaron feels compelled by his own drive to participate and become a valued team player and contributor. It is part of his learning process. Because of his focus and determination, his peers respect him as he drives to be his own person. He no longer acts differently or draw attention to his autism by isolating himself, which was the case during the former years. We encourage and coach this desire that he has to be integrated in the many social settings that he chooses.

We experimented with a sleepover at the house, and I heard comments like "he is pleasantly funny in his own way." The first time we agreed for him to sleep out at a friend's house, he was so excited; the parent was all for it, but then she had that "are you sure" look on her face!

Since then, Aaron has been back several times, and they have come over to his house. It has proven to developmentally enhance communication and socialization in a practical way.

We noticed that sleeping overnight at a friend's house was a good way for our son to connect with kids more advanced than he is as he picked up and adopted good social skills which he could not get at school because he is not always in mainstream. Believe me, it's a scary feeling because the fear of Aaron having a bad experience is always of great concern to us. This has been a risk worth taking based on the very rewarding results we have seen to date.

Children can be unintentionally cruel to each other, so we share the truth in a loving way. Aaron understands that he may not have a lot of friends, true friends, that is, but that's OK! He has learned the value of friendship and rejection in a very real way. He now overcomes rejection with self-confidence. However, the journey must continue, as we try different ways to enhance his skills and expose him to other people who can influence him in a positive way outside of Mom and Dad, the medical staff, and teachers.

I remember that in church he would always sit with both of us, so we decided to have him sit with one of the older brothers. For one year that relationship was up and down and did not go well. But there was a lesson to be learned in that "it takes a village to raise a child with autism." The brother taught him a few things about being socially responsible. It so happened that the brother was promoted, into another position and was not able to sit with Aaron anymore. Because he was so close and respected this gentleman we were concerned that Aaron would not gravitate to anyone else. To our surprise, he now sits with the young men in a socially responsible way. Things have never been the same since that out-of-the-box experience.

On the other hand, being in a self-contained classroom isolates Aaron within his own community. Mainstream programs inside and outside of the school system provides another opportunity to bond with the general population.

Our school district provides many programs that allow kids from the school to come in and tutor basic level, reading, and math. They are called "peer mentors." This is a great program and has been a great addition to Aaron's learning and development experience. Being connected with more advanced students allows him to ramp up on completing assignments and making social connections with other student. This program has also enhanced his speech and articulation skills.

I encourage every special-needs parent to look into this as an option to develop the social, academic, and communication skills of their child. Teachers are at times overwhelmed by larger-than-average class sizes and fewer aides to help bring the most value-added learning experience to the classroom. As a result, the quality of the learning experience sometimes suffers. Having a peer mentor helps on so many levels.

One of our anchor resources is the local Boys and Girls Club of America. The club supports children with special needs through many of their various social and after-school programs, like mentors from the local high schools or colleges who help with homework and other activities.

It has been a great lift for our son to mingle with mainstream children in a non-school environment. The interaction further helps him matriculate socially and developmentally by making new friends, working in teams, and understanding the community he lives in much more holistically. Aaron gets exposed to many other programs he's not involved with at school because he is in a self contained classroom away from the general school population.

The social club is also a great supplemental resource that fills the gap during the many school breaks throughout the year when we need to be at work. He can be at the club for the entire day in a trusted and safe environment.

The kids at the club love Aaron and are very social and respectful. Through this interaction he is now learning what is and is not acceptable in an open society. This is something we struggled to teach effectively at home, probably because we are his parents and it feels like another exercise. Now he accepts and continues to learn the meaning of social acceptability through personal experience with his peers.

Aaron participates in many programs that provide valuable developmental learning experiences which he would not have been exposed to had we not allowed him to participate in not-for-profit community organizations. We had to trust and believe in him, regardless of his condition, having confidence that he would embrace the spirit of the programs and what they offer in terms of structure and support.

As parents we can be well intended but overprotective. I try to protect Aaron from Social acquaintances who make him feel like he does not fit into their group of friends. I have refused to overprotect. So a lot of time is spent on educating some of his peers because they do lack exposure and are unfamiliar with the behaviors, strength, weaknesses and possibilities of children with autism. I realize for the greater good that guiding him and then trusting he will adapt to people and his peers is a big element of his personal development.

I pledged to enjoy this journey with my wife and son. We do everything together. We have taken hundreds of pictures on our many trips and events; we travel the world together, which has given our son a different perspective and view of himself and society that will be with him for the rest of his life. We did not want his life experience to only be one of unending doctor's visits, therapy sessions, and school assignments.

So, what have we learned through this experience? We learned that making time available to enjoy today creates strong family memories and experiences that are very hard to recreate when the opportunity and time has passed. Taking advantage of these opportunities is challenging but helps to pave the way toward a tomorrow in which dreams for our child's future become real, even when the end is not apparent or predictable.

Chapter 7:

KEEP IT SIMPLE

arons spends most of his school day learning with other special needs students. Depending on their diagnosis some are more verbal than others. This impacts the speed at which he would communicate as he started to copy a lot of what he saw in the classroom. Children that are non-verbal use a lot of gestures to communicate. Others use sign language. Aaron is not familiar with that communication style but he would see the hand movement and copy it. He would come home and start a lot of gesturing and making these unfamiliar sounds.

A lot of time has been spent at home correcting the behaviors he picked up from school. We started reading books on communication, sign language, so that he has a better understanding for why it is used. We explained to Aaron that it is important to "use his words" or we would have to send him to a special school to learn sign language to communicate. He did not like that idea. The gestures would go away gradually and then when we lease expected it would reappear. We pushed independent reading of small simple story books, went to the library and got the books with the tapes, so he would listen and read at night. Aaron soon became the class reader and would use those words we tried so hard to get him to express. This simple method creates the results we are looking for Aaron to accomplish and also leverages his reading ability to benefit others in his class.

Keeping it simple does not imply that our kids should not be challenged to stretch beyond their current abilities. Saturday mornings is the day I cut the grass and perform other duties around the house. This is a great opportunity to get Aaron involved and active in helping around the house. We start early so that I can give Aaron the step by step direction and instruction to complete the tasks if he needs it.

I refused to have Aaron sit around while he could have an opportunity to learn and do some small chores around the house. I explained that I have to go outside and clean-up or he would not be able to play outside with his friends because of the mess that would accumulate over time. I prepared him by explaining what we were going to do from the day before. It is easier to ask him to watch me first. After ten minutes I started to ask simple requests like can you pick up the leaves, or get me some extra bags? This became the starting point for him to understand the concept of work. Aaron thought I was having so much fun walking up and down with the lawn mower and blowing the leaves he wanted to try it.

This simple exercise became the starting point for what he would start doing at school to go on to a job-site and perform a variety of job related tasks. The focus of the exercise was to "stay on task." For a special needs child in Aaron's case this principle had to start very early in his life and develop over a long period of time.

Today Aaron works on the coffee cart at school. His responsibility is to go with a teacher to the supermarket, buy the stock and bring it back to school. He has a schedule time when he will travel the hallways collecting the money from the coffee sold. He now likes to think of himself as the banker.

Money skills are not one of his strong points. Actually a teacher at his elementary school said that he just wanted to warn us that Aaron would not be good at any Math related subjects. Not sure who Aaron was being compared to, but I did not see it that way. We purchased math books, books with tapes, and a talking math calculator. The concept of math was still challenging for Aaron to grasp. His godmother purchased an iPad and we nailed basic math, using Apps like: Coin Math, Attainment Dollars and Cents, the piggy bank, were just a few basic programs. Initially I had to push it. Now he independently uses the programs to teach himself without any prompting from me. Aaron is a visual learner, like most children with autism. Abstract thinking and processes does not work for him. If he can visualize what he is being taught or instructed to do, he gets it!

To prove that Aaron is a visual learner I often have to catch myself in mid-sentence while talking with my son. Sometimes I either speak too fast or ask too many questions forgetting that I need to slow down and pace myself so that he fully understands what I am saying, and appropriately formulate his response. When he gives me that blank stare, I either said something incorrectly or I need to repeat myself. As Aaron started building his communication skills he would be dropping off some words like "and, to, they." I could not understand why this was so when the words were in front of him. Speech therapy has helped to overcome a lot of communication challenges. One method was to use picture cards with the words that describe those key words he kept missing. When he missed or skipped over the word, I would show him the card and ask him "what word did you just miss." We would go through the exercise again until he got it. It's a slow but simple process of recognition, memorization and focus through visualization.

I've noticed that Aaron is more challenged to search for an answer to complex requests when put on the spot for a response. Trying to develop the skills denied him by nature is a very challenging and complex endeavor that he has had to endure with great determination and resolve. My wife and I have discovered that sometimes a challenge has to be met with a challenge to drive a specific outcome. Putting Aaron on the spot includes asking him to repeat what he did yesterday. So, you went to school, you had a good day. Tell me about your day? This is not easily repeated back to me in sequential order. To think through the steps of his day is a challenging process. I challenge Aaron to repeat the highlights of his day by asking the same set of questions every day. He realized that I am not going to give up on asking the same set of questions. Repetition is the key to building Aaron's thought process. This is done until I get a consistent response.

There have been occasions we have traveled to another state on our family vacation. I asked Aaron to tell me about the experience, the response is not what I was expecting. However, engaging him in this manner starts a series of thought-provoking questions and mentally engaging conversations between the both of us. We keep it simple by asking Aaron about specific questions like "where did we go yesterday? When did we leave? How long were we away from home? What did you like about the trip, what didn't you like about the trip? He knows what took place during the trip. However, getting him to vocalize his experience is what leads me to putting him on the spot to think about what has taken place and respond accordingly. This is an essential skill. Who knows what happens in life so it is important to give basic details. Aaron has an excellent short and long term memory. Just trying the best I can to get him to verbalize. After many hours the exercise to rehearse the day or event has worked. I will ask him what happened yesterday or today, he will say well mommy went to this store, or daddy did this. He is basically telling on us, but that is OK.

I truly understand the effects of autism, and continue to try my best so that Aaron is better prepared for the future. Aaron can go through the entire day an entire week and not say anything about what happened. I was alarmed and really concerned. Memorizing time and events is another element, which I had to challenge Aaron on. Trying to get him to memorize what time the bus comes to pick him up every morning. What time does the bus get to school? What time does school start? What time does school end. When I asked these questions I got different answers and conflicting times. We would start with the school schedule showing start and end times. I purchased a manual clock that repeats the time to the five minute. We worked through time telling exercises so that he could visually see the time sequence through one of his daily routines. This was important because he has gym late in the evening and needs to remember what time the bus is leaving and prepare himself to be on-time.

Paying attention to how much information Aaron is willing to absorb in one sitting is a good indicator for us to gauge what is appropriate to keep him engaged over an extended period of time. Obviously there is always the attention-deficit issue that can prevent absolute focus.

Sometimes I went overboard or got excited because there was success in the making. Aaron started asking me how my day was. He turned the conversation around and comes to me before I get to him to ask about his day. So I would take advantage of his enthusiasm, by making a request for him to speak to the lunch room attendant at school to get his lunch account balance. I would forget to follow-up and he would not mention it. Lesson learned: always follow-through on a request. When the lunch money is finished Aaron will say the lunch lady said my account needs more money. I was trying all along to get Aaron to be proactive and ask before we got to that point. This effort can easily become counterproductive and backfire into further regression, if there is no consistent follow-through on the request.

I have had to retrain myself to scale down to meet Aaron's needs and level of communication. This has been a personal challenge for me to unwind years of learned methods of communication.

Caution is an important element in the act of challenging our child, because enthusiasm without temperance can destroy good intentions. I am now very cautious about getting too motivated or liberal in my enthusiasm, and about applying a lot of instructions and information in one sitting. This is my best effort to keep things simple for my son. I have learned that it is so essential to recognize the importance and balance of a positive experience that includes challenging him without overwhelming him. This keeps his level of motivation high so that he can feel compelled to challenge himself and push beyond his comfort zone.

In my professional life I have a refined set of methods such as asking questions requiring an executive summary. Sometimes a yes and no response will do and other times hitting high level points and recommendations get me the information I need. This is an effective tool I use to extract information and certain responses from people I interact with on a daily basis. Sometimes my professional communication style carries over during conversations with Aaron. This communication style does get in the way of simplifying my interaction efforts with Aaron. It has served me well because of my training but, can be a barrier, because the expectation is so different. The focus is now changed from getting Aaron to understand me to me understanding his communication style and developing that. Sometimes it meant saying things differently, like if I would say "I thought we agreed," would be changed to "do you remember!"

My son has taught me to think differently about my approach and motivation to get results. At times he will often try to respond in the best way he can when I have slipped into my old way of getting things done by using learned skills to influence change. When he starts to struggle I realize I need to change my approach. This continues to be an ongoing experience and discovery process for both of us.

Simplicity and consistency works for Aaron. It can

be challenging for me to switch my communication style from being a professional to coming down to a level that is productive and meaningful to engage Aaron. To understand rather than to be understood works very well for Aaron. I have found many advantages to this technique, which is evidenced by his ability to now ask who, what, and why questions. When I realize we are making progress, the frustration level starts to diminish on both sides of the fence.

Aaron is no more in an uncomfortable place. This is a continual learning experience for all of us. We continue to refine this communication process at home and in the community. It starts with how to react to Mom, Dad, teacher, and friends when put in uncommon and varying situations, for example he was asked do you have any food allergies? That can be very awkward for a child with autism, especially when the message is not clear and the response is out of context. This is where I recommend patience. So instead of answering for him I explained what a food allergy is, and then asked do you have an allergy, Aaron said no to the lady asking the question.

This is the reality of the world we live and function in. Mom and Dad will not always be around. How should we prepare our child with autism for this inevitable situation to get the best outcomes during his lifetime? Should we hold back, or should we be smart?

How far should we go to expose our child with autism who is living in a safe and loving trusted environment that can sometimes be far removed from the blinding reality of the world outside the home?

It becomes necessary to rehearse and follow through on real-life experiences that are an inevitable encounter for Aaron once he leaves the confines of his home to work and socialize with the world around him. As adults we already have experienced uncomfortable challenges at some point in our lives. We understand the discomfort and the pain. Now imagine a child with autism in the same situation. The need for coaching and mentoring becomes very real and an important requirement to be as well prepared as possible.

Sometimes I have to look to friends for help and comfort when caught in an embarrassing life situations especially when I am unprepared to give a response. My reaction time may not be as spontaneous to respond accordingly or to express what I think in the moment.

I am acutely aware how my son must feel when he cannot respond spontaneously. With this in-mind it is easier for me to be very sensitive to his communication needs. I am committed to do whatever it takes so that he is prepared to the best of his ability. I can therefore help our son make good choices and understand the consequences of bad choices in the real world. Keeping it simple but real has become a practical matter for us as we create and think of different model situations to practice at home. Knowing "how should he react" in a given situation does not come naturally for Aaron; it has to be learned. We are making great progress just by putting this experiment to the test.

We've worked very hard to resist the urge to think for Aaron or put words in his mouth, even when we're just trying to help! It is better and more productive for him to use his own words. Evidently, we consistently provide small prompts to get his thinking process lined up. However, the goal is to get him to think as much as possible for himself.

Aaron often takes his time going through the process of thinking even though nothing seems to be falling in place for him. Children with autism so often become stunned during the thinking process, like a deer caught in headlights, seeing the light but not being able to react and respond appropriately with spontaneity. In these instances my wife and I have learned to "dim the light." We try very hard to spend a fair amount of time challenging Aaron to take on more decisions, sharpen his thought process, and expand his capabilities just because he shows strong signs of expanding those abilities.

Challenging our son by asking direct questions when he says something that is not quite clear proved to be very effective. We have discovered that by asking direct questions like "what do you mean?" and not being afraid to say, "I don't quite understand you," helps him to search for an alternative response to clarify his statement. It works every time when we put him in a position where he needs to be clear. This has proved to us that we needed to adjust our way of interacting with our son to get the best results.

It has not been an easy experience. Aaron would say things and then change his mind in an instant. We soon discovered that he needs time and space so he can get comfortable with his decisions, rather than just reacting because he wants to be spontaneous. I'd rather he think and react than be spontaneously wrong. Many times we have tried so hard to resist the temptation to micromanage our expectations for him.

There is a delicate balance between not doing enough and doing too much. Experience has taught us that some endeavors can become counterproductive, as our anxiousness to see our son succeed turn into anxiety for us and frustrates the objective.

As we started scaling back, giving him some time to adjust his thinking, he started to reciprocate more and take the initiative in many different areas. When we were driving, he would start trying to read street signs and memorize certain aspects of his environment. This was very encouraging. He continues to engage through dialogue and conversation, and we can't keep him quiet now!

Our relationship as a family has elevated to a point where Aaron initiates tasks on his own. He asks to vacuum the house or cut the lawn. My wife and I let him lead the way. He needed to adopt the feeling of empowerment to make his own decisions, to learn and grow.

We came to a point when it was necessary to turn down our expectations which momentarily provided the opportunity for Aaron to grow and develop with less prompting and pushing because we just could not see the danger of constantly keeping the spotlight on him. Now he welcomes our help without feeling blinded by it, and we are all less frustrated through this development process.

Aaron taking the initiative is a dream comes true for all of us. We are so proud of him. He managed the pressure very well to get to this stage.

Over a six-year period we noticed some strong developmental trends and personalities coming through that have been very encouraging and positive.

Aaron is now emerging in the areas of speech and language, cognitive processing, socialization, and independence. These four abilities enable Aaron to exceed prior significant delays and overcome the many barriers presented by autism.

As the barriers standing in the way of those four abilities come down, his potential to advance has increased beyond our expectations. It appears that after being held back it is time for him to release his true potential by trying harder, being more determined and giving his all if a task is too challenging for him. This is a quality that has emerged because we essentially slowed down to meet his pace of development by keeping our interactions with him very simple and specific. Now Aaron is coming into his own being very determined and having a chatty and jovial personality trait about him.

We soon discovered that while working inside these four development windows that things do not always go according to plan. There is always an element of surprise, such as regression over holiday and vacation periods. We had to balance extracurricular activities with maintaining consistency during breaks and extended holidays. Requesting that the school provide an extended school year has stopped Aaron from further regression during long holiday breaks. The extended school curriculum in Math and English kept Aaron focused and on track for the new school year.

The very thought of regression always reminds us that whatever unique method we come up with, it is not an exact science; it's an experiment. We see what works in a given situation and never feel guilty about failure. Our mindset is that nothing beats failure but a try. We scale up and down as the need arises, but the routine is essential to actively keep our son engaged. This is all part of our deliberate effort to keep it simple!

Educating family and friends helped them to also follow through on what we had put in place to get the best results from their interactions with our son. We have made it easy for them by sharing our experiences, and the outcomes are inspiring for all.

Understanding Aaron's stages of development also gave us the head start we so desperately needed and enabled us to seek out and find the right resources and tools such as timely information and community support beginning with our church. Being around other people has developed his people skills, which were very poor. Now he is a people person. We fully engage ourselves in his development by providing the appropriate environment for him to have a rich and well rounded life being exposed to athletic and recreational activities. Aaron gladly participates in the regular stuff that boys like to do with fathers. We went to see a monster truck show and an ice hockey game. I was told that children with autism hate crowds and noise. It was a great experience. Aaron loved it so much he keeps asking when are we going back.

Aaron has a special area that is dedicated for him to do his academic work at home. This area mimics his classroom setting in the home environment and is the only place in the house that when we go in there it's all work-time. It is such a great environment for us to provide him with the help and support he needs. His teachers are noticing the result of this extra help he is getting at home.

Overall Aaron makes progress in reading, math, cognitive thinking, and overall social behavior and adaptability to his environment. We are talking about a child who started out with zero social skills, could not hold a conversation beyond one minute, and was very distant in terms of not socializing with his peers or anyone at all. He avoided people in general. With a very low IQ well below fifty none of the other family members kids wanted to connect with him, because he was not considered smart enough. We would go out to family events or social gatherings and we would have to leave early because Aaron was bored and disruptive. He felt that he did not fit in. That was then. We are glad about the progress he is making right now. The dream for full development of Aaron's ability is forming and taking shape!

Each time we learned something new and applied the experience, it has fundamentally helped to normalize our family over the disruptive years. This is a life-changing experience for our family. We believe in our son and his abilities; there is no such thing as the impossible.

Aaron has exceeded our most basic expectation for him to be able to communicate, share his feelings, and be friendly and loving over a short period of time. He has progressed far beyond the timeframe we were looking for him to mature over the next five to ten year period in reading math and athletics.

Aaron has grown from doing single tasks to variable tasks like cleaning, doing the laundry, shredding the unwanted mail, doing his homework and vacuuming in one day. He is being strongly influenced by this new multitasking skill to continue improving at his own pace in his own time.

Creating small stretch goals over time was a good barometer to assess and test Aaron's true potential to be his best. The stretch goals started out as simple as writing a sentence then writing a paragraph then writing a chapter. This is an experiment we have now proved to be a worthwhile exercise with profound results. It helped with keeping Aaron on task for an extended period of time he became more focused and started asking for help when it was appropriate. Previously he used to just sit there until I came over to ask how he was doing only to find out he had stopped working. Now he has been trained to ask for help. This has carried over into school where he will ask for help because he wants to learn. The success of Aaron's continued development is tied to using simple communication skills and relevant resources ranging from use of iPad devices, books tapes and finding that delicate balance between doing too much and not doing enough.

CHAPTER 8:

EARLY INTERVENTION

The facts are boys out number girls with autism five to one. In the most recent survey, children with autism have increased by 78 percent from over a decade ago. One in fifty-four boys are being diagnosed with autism in the US. Globalize that, and the numbers are staggering. Do not discount the advice of friends and family members, who might recognize the signs of autistic activity first, just because they are not as close to your child as you are. Start by asking a lot of questions, and never treat good information as being suspect. Take every piece of information in good faith. Go in with an open mind and eyes wide open.

I have always tempered my approach with caution, good information, and doing my own homework. Sometimes doctors will agree straight out the gate with what you are seeing in your child's development. Others you will need to convince, or you may need to seek a second or even third opinion for validation purposes. I've learned the value of being, vigilant not complacent. This has worked for our family. It may work differently for other fathers in the same situation. I try to be smart about my actions and reactions to what I think and what I know. I have to live with the fact that when the rubber meets the road, I made the best selection from a choice of alternatives for my son.

I realized through being exposed to autism that I really did not know as much as I thought I did. The entire process is a new learning experience, and it is hard to appreciate unless it is lived and challenged every day. It took me a while to appreciate what our family was presented with. I had to disengage myself from my former thinking. Once I got over the hump of disbelief, I was on my way to make this experience the best one possible for our son.

Early intervention was the beginning point for me. I never appreciated the value of early intervention until my wife explained it to me a couple of times. The general rule of early intervention for children with autism is "the earlier, the better." When in doubt, get your child diagnosed! Embark on an early intervention plan as soon as possible. This has been our motto from day one. We started pretty early, and it has been an uphill challenge from the beginning. I cannot imagine what the situation for Aaron would have been like without early intervention. We were very fortunate to catch on to his condition at the earliest possible opportunity.

My idea of early intervention was very limited. Sending Aaron to therapies and developing an IEP for him with the school just about summed up my level of understanding about early intervention. My wife demonstrated to me that I was so wrong. The better approach is to invest personal time and start the intervention process at home. The external professional help is a supplement so that Aaron has the best of both worlds. This approach makes sense because more hours are spent at home than at the therapist.

Early intervention is about doing a lot of homework to build awareness, then turning around and doing the work to make it come together in a meaningful and practical way. I soon discovered that an unsuccessful early intervention program relies too heavily on the limited hours spent with the professional external help and not enough time spent at home reinforcing the principles and techniques provided by the therapists. A lot of the learning steps that I thought were so rudimentary I had to repeatedly rehearse again and again. It really is hands-on all the time, even when I did not have the energy and sometimes the patience for it. Fathers can overcome the feeling of frustration by just stepping back go for a long drive, walk or just do something else to change the focus. Early intervention is not an event you wait for to happen; it is a step that you have to have a plan around so that you can hit those critical milestones.

There is early intervention that comes from

enlisting professional testing services to determine age appropriate skills and behaviours. Being proactive and taking action to evaluate Aaron sooner than later provided us with some peace of mind and actually starts the process to target those developmentally weak areas which take time to correct. Time is of the essence to get the maximum benefit from an early intervention approach. Early intervention should never be a reactive process after family and friends convince us that there is a problem. Believe me, that is the moment that a lot of mistakes are made, because parents go to the first doctor, therapist, psychologist, specialist and we forget to get a second opinion to verify what we have been told. Always trust, but verify!

Essentially, early intervention is the interruption of delays in patterns of growth and development which is not consistent for the child's age. The goal of the service is to provide the support in correcting deficiencies that impact learning and development. Research has documented that early intervention is critically important and is best engaged during a very short window of time for maximum results.

In that short window of time, there are so many elements that have to be nurtured and attended to. We did not have a clue at the beginning of this process! A lot of our efforts were ineffective. On many occasions we just had to rely on word of mouth from other parents in our network. Sometimes it was just plain good fortune that we met the right people at the right time.

Some examples of taking advantage of early intervention opportunities for Aaron included finding a good speech and language pathologist and occupational therapist that works extensively and primarily with children with autism. Finding a pediatrician is very important to build history with treating Aaron. This became fundamental since he will be spending most of his developmental years with this caregiver. Aaron was five years old when we started to see significant changes in his social interaction and language development.

Early intervention helped establish a sound foundation for improving his overall growth in speech and behavior development goals. He became much more comfortable and confident about himself and about delivering on what was being expected of him. As new unsocial behaviors emerged, I quickly drew on lessons learned from past behavior management and learning development techniques such as taking away privileges as needed, restating the expectations and reinforcing them until new behaviors are adopted, identifying the undesirable behavior is a technique used by the therapists to improve Aarons overall capabilities to first understand that there is a problem which needs to be addressed.

Every parent we met through the autism parent network became another opportunity to introduce someone to the benefits of early intervention. Most parents came into the network after receiving a diagnosis on their child. We promoted early intervention as a tool and technique to everyone who would listen. We could not wait to share our success with others. Who would have thought I would find myself doing that? I didn't want other parents to go through the hard experience that my wife and I went through. Now our son has a great foundation to build on.

The best gift we could ever provide to our son was early intervention. Had we not started as soon as possible, we would still be dealing with some of the inherent delays we have been struggling with since early childhood. Early intervention results in the increase of developmental gains, long-term skills improvements, and adaptation to appropriate social norms.

Early intervention is an expensive endeavor that requires a tremendous amount of time and resources to get the best results. By the time we had finished fighting with the insurance company, our son still started a bit late on his early intervention program. In our opinion, it is so important to start intervention support services like Easter Seals and Oasis as soon as a diagnosis is made if there are no barriers or restrictions from the insurance companies.

Some insurance companies will not start payment until the child is in an active therapy or care program, thus delaying the entire process, especially if family funds are not readily available to go private. Early intervention is not about finding just anyone to work with or support our child but finding someone with a passion for this line of work. Early intervention has to be more than a paycheck for them. We have been down that road and suffered with very little satisfaction for the time and investment made. It was an expensive and painstakingly slow learning experience.

Finding an early intervention therapist took us awhile longer than expected, as we had to go through a series of events to build a case validating our son's need for treatment. I know I am preaching to the choir here, for most parents of children with autism have come up against this challenge. Meeting the insurance requirements was a continuous mountain of paperwork and endless phone calls. This is against the backdrop of having what I would consider very good insurance coverage.

The only advice that I can offer fathers, mothers, and caregivers when dealing with insurance companies is to never let up on the gas. The insurance hurdles have been one of the major challenges we've had to overcome. Insurance hurdles are the main reasons why many parents take longer than necessary to maximize the benefits of a well-developed early intervention program for their child with autism. After overcoming the restrictions and limitations placed on entitlement to services we just decided to max out the insurance limits by putting our son in as many early intervention programs as were available without overloading him. Don't give the insurance a reason to limit your child's benefits just because you did not utilize all the allocated sessions provided through your insurance.

Our approach from the beginning was to put in all the necessary time to make the medical programs work to our son's advantage, especially after having to fight so hard for them in the first place. Every available dollar under the plan was put to work. We left nothing on the table! Looking back, we are so glad we did what we had to do on a tight budget. Today that little extra effort has paid off tremendously.

Occupational therapy, physical therapy, speech and language, and social development were the four areas we targeted. We adapted our schedules to our son's needs. These four windows of opportunity were the key to his long-term development. It was challenging from the beginning, but we have not ceased to keep building on those four pillars.

Another lesson we learned through this process was the importance of having all current and past medical records and historical data in one place. Nothing is more frustrating than not having the required medical data at hand. If you move, it is essential and necessary to get copies of your child's records. If you don't, your child's prior medical provider may not always return your call in a timely manner or furnish the correct information. This happened to us. If we had requested these records before moving, it would have made the transition from one therapist to another easier.

Because of a lack of adequate medical data, some therapists wanted to make their own evaluation, which resulted in more cost to us and could have been avoided.

We had to challenge their requests because this kind of rework took a lot of valuable therapy time away from Aaron.

Finding a good occupational therapist, physical therapist and a strong speech and language pathologist who could work with our son was a challenge in itself. Not all therapists are equal! Some perform the basic requirements, while others go above and beyond because they are passionate about their work with children experiencing these deficits. Some therapists truly go the extra mile because they care. Other times we experienced the production-line effect of being pushed through the in-out process; it was a genuine waste of our time and effort. However, we did learn that we needed to trust our instincts and good judgment when selecting a therapist or caregiver for our son.

Aaron found it very difficult to cooperate and take direction from people outside of the immediate family. His desire to cooperate depended heavily on the chemistry and trust between Aaron and his therapist. Just settling for the first one out of the insurance book was not adding value and ended up delaying his development. We have experienced better results from therapists who see their patients as customers. We have experienced great results living by one rule in this area: do the research and ask the right questions. Searching for a therapist is no different from working with people I do business with, commune with at church, or socialize with in my networks of friends and associates.

In general, I am always looking for that special chemistry with people I work and live with on a daily basis. Aaron has the same expectation requirement and is indifferent to anything else. So we went through a couple of uncomfortable relationships before we found the right individuals. It is never about the organization that they work for; it is more about their personalities. We have discovered after many attempts that the right therapist knows how to be firm yet professional and flexible to our son's complex learning and development challenges.

Some other behavior challenges tied to speech and language deficiencies prevented cooperation with the specialists. Here again, a lot of redirection, handholding, and being sensitive to Aaron's needs had to take place over time. Our son went through a phase of repetitive ticks and self-indulging behaviors. This was apparent if he was disinterested in the caregiver. Behavior modification has been a slow and painful process for all of us. Today most of these behaviors and symptoms have fully abated.

Now that we have passed over many of the inhibiting behaviors, other opportunities have emerged to help form Aaron's character by sharpening his personality, individuality, and mindset. Getting our son focused and exposed to art, science, various social settings, and extracurricular activities has been helpful to build team spirit, develop greater synergies with his peers, foster the ability to participate in team events, and bond and socialize with different people at all levels. We are now seeing him develop an awareness that did not exist before. He is aware of a world outside himself and his place in it. This success is attributed to our focus on early intervention.

Fathers can be very influential to help our autistic child form stronger social skills. These skills are the prerequisites for developing lifelong friendships. We were concerned about simple things like Aaron being ignored, unaccepted, overwhelmed, and frustrated. Simple things like using the restroom needed to be well thought out. Thankfully the kids embraced him. I remembered one day I went to pick him up, and as we left he was saying good-bye to some of the kids and teachers by first name. This was the beginning of a positive social change for him.

Continuing the trend and keeping a child with autism engaged is one of the unique challenges. Parents just don't have a lot of spare time. I have taken Aaron to cooking classes to keep him engaged. Using his hands to make things helped him to stay focused and on task. The library is a great place to keep him engaged. They are always having theater and children book reading events. In my local community we have an organization called Horizon. They have teamed up with another organization called Golden Soldiers. Golden Soldiers is a nonprofit church group of young people working tremendously with the special needs community. They have free movie days where the entire theater is booked out for the special needs community to watch a movie with family and friends.

Aaron gets very bored and distracted very easily. We dedicated 100 percent of our disposable time to manage and better engage him in social activities like focus, which is a non-profit organization providing social events, cooking classes and is a good environment to connect with other children in a non-intimidating environment. The structure and support provided by focus is one of the great supplemental programs for children with autism.

The social development results have been astounding. Now it is possible even with the onset of prevailing developmental delays that our child, like yours will exceed expectations. This is something that every parent of a child with autism looks forward to with great expectation and anticipation. Believe me, there is no such thing as a case of autism that is hopeless.

Aaron has started to excel academically, socially, and developmentally. This improvement is at his own pace and ability and he keeps on gaining new ground by overcoming those disorders which have been a part of his life. His success is put in contrast to where he is coming from and the barriers he has overcome which we attribute to early intervention. This is another reason for us to celebrate. His performance and behavior have exceeded our greatest expectation for him. I used to feel I was building my son's future on false hopes because I could not see past autism; I could not anticipate the end from this vantage point. Our son has proved me wrong in this instance and will probably prove me wrong again.

So, if you find yourself behind on any of the occupational therapy, physical therapy, speech and language, and social development goals and milestones, it is never late to get engaged; this only means that you will need additional time and effort to get the same results as someone who started the process earlier.

If at all possible I have tried using private therapy as a supplement to insurance covered programs. The idea is to get all the sessions that the insurance will pick-up, then when the insurance stops pick up with private sessions. Private sessions prevent service gaps during ongoing therapy. Sometimes family members can be a great resource. When all is said and done, lean on the school system. Every little bit counts toward your child maximizing every available opportunity to advance.

Pursuing all the available channels to address my son's needs is an exercise that is intense and very demanding, with slow results. However, I can assure you that I am thankful for the action taken now. I see a reduction in my stress level because it gets a little easier to manage Aaron's busy schedule.

The results will be different for each child and parent. Every child's autistic situation is unique. However, the outcomes are similar because the ultimate goal of every father is that our children succeed through strong growth patterns, maturity to be the best they can be, and become as independent as their abilities will permit.

Aaron demands a lot of our time. I had to scale down on a lot of community activities which I was involved in to accommodate his schedule. I have no regrets about all the hours and effort put into early intervention to get Aaron to where he needs to be. Some of these sessions were far from where I live. I am so glad that I took advantage of the opportunity to fully utilize the therapist and available tools and services over the years.

We discovered later that Aaron needed another type of specialist help related to his growth. This was not related to autism, but the impact was just as severe, because we had a very small window of time to react. There is no information or studies to show that autism and low growth are linked. We did the research and discovered that his growth plates were not developing properly. This led us to an endocrinologist. I mention this development because if we were aware what was going on we could have started much earlier and Aaron would have benefitted from a couple extra inches in his growth development.

This is another example of what early intervention can do for a child. When we started Aaron on the growth therapy he only had three years of growth before the bones would start to fuse; all growth ends at that point, so there was a rush to get him on "growth hormones." However, we were uncomfortable about the side effects, even though we did the research; I guess not knowing anybody else who used hormones accelerated our discomfort levels. We were skeptical about the idea of another round of injections and shots. However, we started at a low dosage and moved on from there. Aaron has about one year left before the growth plate stops, and we're comfortable that he'll have a good height for his age.

The takeaway is that every form of early intervention is important, even if it is unrelated to autism. This is more evident as the windows of opportunities are narrow and close very quickly.

As a parent raising a child with autism, I take comfort in the fact that Aaron bonds with other children he has met at the therapist office. I and my wife have made new friends. We bond very closely with parents through sharing information, just listening to their concern and frustration and spending time together. Autism has become the common bond of our friendship.

CHAPTER 9

THE BOND

I have a very busy schedule that keeps me engaged on a daily basis. Bonding is not just for Aaron, it was important for me also. Bonding is not another way for me to spend as much quality time with my son. It is my role and responsibility as a father to connect and be engaged. Bonding has helped to shape my experiences and character by being more patient and supportive to Aaron's relationship needs that he is not fully capable of expressing verbally.

Our family has met some great children, their parents and caregivers over the many years that Aaron has been doing therapy and special activities. These families have made a big impact on our lives. Our son may be higher functioning but he goes out of his way to be their friend and to make sure that they are OK. I remember we went to a musical that was just for kids with autism and their parents/caregivers. There were a lot of different behaviors going on. Aaron would go up to the other children and say hello my name is Aaron what is yours!

Aaron would reach out to many of the children and offer to help where needed and when appropriate. I have spent a lot of time at the various Special Olympics training sessions and events. It is just amazing to see the support and cooperation being displayed between different families from different backgrounds. Aaron has bonded very well with many children he has met through Special Olympics. It has been a great place for our family to develop lasting friendships with families we have just met and bonded with. It is so easy to bond by willingly sharing unsolicited information with parents of a child on the autism spectrum.

A wonderful parent of a child with autism said to me that she had a big house and wanted to invite Aaron over with other kids to camp out in her backyard for the weekend. What an inspirational act of selfless kindness and thoughtfulness!

The idea was good enough to get us to start thinking in this direction. It was very possible for our son to venture out in this manner if only we could get some minor ground rules in place as a guideline. This was a first step to demonstrating Aaron's independence and willingness to bond with other children in the autism community.

Aaron is an only child so the exposure to other children and families in the autism community has worked wonders for him. He has learned to share, care about others, having others care about him. Learning to be nice and thoughtful is a great way for Aaron to bond with his peers and adults. I learned to let go and stop being overly in control of the situation so that he would bond with others outside the family circle. I learned from his willingness to be a friend and bond with others when it was not required for him to do so.

I thought I was doing a lot of bonding with Aaron, but when I saw Aaron reach out to others, I realized I can do much more to bond with Aaron and other children and families with autism. Bonding with Aaron has come through learning experiences and making some mistakes like doing more of the things he likes and making it something we can do together. It took me a while to play games with him. Through this we became closer and more dependent on each other. I would do the reading and he would show me how to navigate the control.

At first I tried to bond with Aaron using my past bonding experiences. The bonding I had in mind was like bonding with my football buddies. We all talk the same language of sports, and even when we disagree in a competitive sporting environment, we are still friends. Bonding with my son was so much different from what I thought it needed to be. I had to reshape my thinking and approach.

There was something unique about this experience that I could not quite put my finger on. It was special.

Just to get a smile and a hug was worth the time and patience. I also noticed that bonding worked better if I was not always directing and allowed my son to lead the way. It was not for me to dictate the terms. Bonding comes in many forms; it's what two people make it!

In the back of my mind I had to remember that the moment for bonding was not always at my convenience, but at Aaron's prompting. Prompting could be as varied as going to the local entertainment facility or as simple as playing a game and watching how much he could mercilessly beat me at basketball. Most times it was just a matter of presence and flexibility. Just being there for him was enough in his mind!

I remember one particular weekend when our family watched an animated movie together. At the end, when the credits and background music came on, Aaron started to dance to the music and called to me to join him. Was I up to it? No. Did I do it? Yes. I was reluctant after a long day on the job. However, he persisted so we both started dancing. To my surprise, he started to say, "Go, Aaron!" I laughed so hard.

Take every opportunity to bond that presents itself. It may come when you are not at your highest motivational point to participate. Make the effort; it's only a small window of time that's not to be missed.

My wife and I are always thinking of new things to help us continue to bond on different levels. Bonding continues to provide structure and helps Aaron to understand the value of long-term relationships that he will have a better chance of managing as he grows up. I've been surprised by his ongoing requests to go out more often and do more stuff, just like a regular child. I will confess that I'm not very good at PlayStation, or the Game boy, for that matter. My son beats me every time. But getting beaten is not the focus; this presents another reason and another opportunity to bond. Aaron is learning with this the value of growing up in a competitive world where there are winners and losers.

The most valuable lesson Aaron has learned is not to be afraid to challenge and be challenged. Backing away from a challenge is an easy option for most of us, but he seldom takes that path because he has had to challenge himself in a big way. We kept emphasizing the need to keep trying if failure persists. For Aaron this is a learned behavior to which he has adapted very well.

Making the sacrifice outside a very busy work and church schedule is very important for both of us as parents. Aaron knows that Dad and Mom work extra hard to fit everything in. We golf, swim, play basketball, go mountain climbing, bike riding, speech, occupational therapy, karate, visit the local GameStop to play the latest games and check on our elderly neighbor. We do it all with just enough time to sleep!

Again, we never lose sight of the reality that time is of the essence, and there is such a very small window of time to work from. All the sacrifice and effort leads us toward bringing our son closer to his dream, or as near as possible to a "normal life."

The bonding experience has really pulled us closer as a family when all the other pressures were taking their toll. Our bonding has matured to a state where we do not have to say a lot. We just enjoy each moment. I couldn't ask for anything else. I'm just very grateful to be in this spot at this point of his maturity cycle.

We still have challenges with speech and language and the conceptualizing of certain material, but progress is being made every day. We have a goal, and we are tracking to get there. Bonding has by far increased Aaron's social ability and interaction on many fronts. He continues to be master over his inabilities. Bonding has allowed Aaron to build self-confidence, character, and the ability to overcome much of the indifference because his ideas do not come over clear to the person listening as a result of his communication weaknesses which are improving. We continue to develop the remaining challenges so that he can be confident in expressing his feelings and emotions. This is something that children with autism do not do very well.

Socialization and bonding with mainstream and children on the autism spectrum has become a catalyst for our son to overcome a lot of self-doubt and development delays. He now has friends who care about him

Bonding with others has turned into a great opportunity to better manage his behaviors that would not be acceptable or tolerable outside the social community of autism. I'm confident that the other delays and deficiencies will diminish over time as he emerges from the shadow of autism. We are confident that he's on the right path to being the best he can be.

I will never lose hope and never stop dreaming for my child to reach his full potential. Children with autism thrive on praise and a strong support structure. Not just my child—I have witnessed countless others who have emerged or are emerging from the grasp of autism. If we give up, then who is going to care if our children succeed or fail?

My wife consistently reinforces the value of being happy and comfortable in your own skin. Despite the challenges in his life, Aaron knows that we love him. Children with autism will always go the extra mile and try harder to exceed your expectations when they feel secure. As parents we have learned that it takes time and patience to see and enjoy the fruits of our labor of love. For us this is really the bottom line. When impatience and frustration start to dominate our natural expectations for our son, we have to pull back and remind ourselves that we are on a journey. Once I got comfortable with that mind-set, we were on a roll!

Reprioritizing on short notice really helped me to do all that I could to build a strong relationship as father and son. I used to travel a lot, but traveling is not that important anymore; I use technology to successfully do my job. This flexibility gives me more time to be present on a daily basis, which continues to strengthen our bonding relationship and has helped me to overcome doubts and frustrations that became barriers, standing in the way of our friendship, our growth together, and our communication. Now I am part of the changes and improvements and not just hearing about them.

For me the bonding experience has been unique and very rewarding. I'm not at all sure if the level of success we enjoy would be as progressive had it not been for good bonding. Good bonding provides the foundation for great experiences. Great experiences really help to bridge some social and behavior gaps created by autism. I have noticed in Aaron's case that bonding is transferrable into the arena of his personal and social life.

I have learned to do a lot of research on the Web for outdoor camps and activities that he does not have an opportunity to participate in at school because he is not fully in mainstream. There are so many clubs and social activities that cater to children with autism in our local community. If there are families with special-needs children, then there are activities to support this special community to further connect and bond. Many communities provide services and opportunities to meet, greet, and bond with other kids and parents in the special-needs community. Parents have become very savvy at extending the bond outside the immediate family circle. This made it possible for our son to understand that he is not alone on this journey.

We have made it our mission to provide Aaron with those life experiences and connections to his wider community. We believe that making those connections to bond socially is very important. It also gives us peace of mind that he recognizes he is not alone. As his parents we are aware that we have no monopoly on the future. So we prepare daily by advocating on his behalf and making those connections that are in his best long-term interest.

CHAPTER 10

THE ESSENCE
OF ADVOCACY

A dvocacy as I now know it after years of trial and error is all about "making those relationships work!" After finding the right connections between available resources and other untapped opportunities capable of providing the best available services to support our son's development, we know advocacy works for us. Advocacy is not a social event or a waste of time. On the contrary, it is time well spent as information is shared and resources become available. Most of the information and resources we have access to have come from the efforts of our advocacy.

Advocacy yields great results and outcomes. It has really enriched our son's life. Many times we have gone it alone; other times we have solicited the help and influence of other like-minded parents or caregivers to make our point. Nobody listens if we stay silent. It is always necessary and beneficial to make a lot of noise and create some waves, especially in this economic environment when services are being cut and agencies are persistently stating that there is a lack of federal and local funding sources for major programs. There is no shame in having a meltdown when advocating for your child's benefit becomes personal. My experience is that no one takes an advocate seriously if you are afraid to push very hard!

Take charge and actively pursue all the right resource channels to secure every possible benefit for your child. I have pushed for my child even when I was being labeled a nuisance, because I was like a dog with a bone, very unwilling to let go, until they came through for Aaron. This has occurred many times when we were trying to get approval for the Katie Becket waiver and when the school needed to make a reasonable accommodation for extended school year services over the summer holiday period for Aaron.

I and my wife are relentless advocates, even though there were times when the pursuit was becoming impossible and things were not happening as we expected. But we refused to take no for an answer. A no-nonsense approach helped us to get ahead with government agencies and school districts. I will be honest; parents need to have thick skin to take the rejection and wasting time that comes with being an advocate for a child with autism.

Aaron has been with us when we had to negotiate with authorities and he has seen firsthand the significance of fighting for your rights for services. Some of this speaking up for what you need has rubbed off on him. Aaron tries to exercise the negotiation side of advocacy when he needs something from us he starts to emphasize his position and does not give in that easily. I realize advocacy is a transferrable skill. Once you apply it and taste the results of success, it's hard not to always lead the charge against federal, state, or local organizations that keep shedding resources and support services for children and adults with autism.

Our first attempt to be advocates was disastrous because we did not have a clue about how to approach it. Fathers can be very influential in situations like this. Some of the steps I used to correct prior mistakes included requesting an appointment with the person at the top not the customer services staff. Not being afraid to complain that we were getting the run around when it was warranted. Kept a ledger of contact names, amount of visits, communications and lastly records of all materials sent including faxed transmittals. Another important piece of advice is to really be specific about what you want them to-do. Most social services and school distinct personal have very low tolerance for the long story. Get straight to the point.

After a couple of tries, we became more focused and aware of how to get our point across and push for the results we need in a professional manner. It is so easy to get ugly when things do not go as planned and there's an apparent lack of cooperation. Developing a resistance to the word no and having a thick skin to counteract rejection can be an asset. Rejection is the gateway to getting what we need to support our child's growth and development. Lesson learned: nobody cares if you don't succeed, so I constantly remind myself that getting personal without getting ugly gets results. I vowed that my child would not become another budget-cut statistic. Experience has shown me that there is an alternative way if I dig deep enough.

I have spent a substantial amount of time networking and advocating at every social and community event both inside and outside my postal code. Wherever the network exists, and if there is an advantage to help our son or another family, we always make the effort to turn the travel to and from these destinations into a family day or night out. Eat pizza and shop on the way there and back home.

As I continued with advocacy, I learned about so many different opportunities. For example, my wife and I never used to know that there are nonprofit organizations and churches that sponsor tennis and baseball camps for children with special needs. We discuss all opportunities with Aaron to get his feedback and identify his interest level. If he says yes, we are all over it. If it requires money, we spend our own, and there are other agencies, both private and public, including social services, that will pay as discussed in chapter twelve the financial impact of Autism. It is more expensive in the long term not to provide these services for our children if they are denied the opportunity and experience to become active community and civic members. Again, if the local community fails, we find another resource. Our initial approach is to get at the free benefits first, and then use our own money as a last resort, so that our child enjoys the best experiences possible.

Winning at advocacy is a powerful motivator. We send strong messages to Aaron that failure does not always have to be acceptable. In our parent network, we work with each other for a common goal, to win for our children with special needs by giving them a chance to progress, develop, and thrive independently!

This is one of the practical ways that our son understands the value of persistence and not always giving in to someone even when you are flatly told no. This insight shows up in new behaviors that he is forming—when I say no, he comes back at me, and he loves it. Advocacy has enabled us to leverage the knowledge and insight of others. This is why this section of the book is so relevant. It is very important, as everything we do for our son hangs on the ability to effectively and aggressively advocate.

Everyone in our family genuinely wants to help; we believe in the power of taking the first initiative. There are people and organizations with the ability to make this journey so much easier and lighter for parents, but these organizations do not advertise themselves, and they will not come knocking on your door. If you want it, you must go and get it.

The keys to advocacy are consistency and persistence. Private and public enterprises want to be good stewards in the communities they serve. If there's a program you would like that is not available in your general area, advocacy is a path to getting support from these organizations. There is always an organization with the means and the heart to support our efforts and help us along the way. This is how the Special Olympics and Autism Speaks got started. You are not alone. Don't let frustration and anxiety make you give up! Keep advocating for your child.

Working with the school system, doctors, specialists, and government agencies for special-needs children can become a very painful experience. My wife has run into many challenges and obstacles that stood in the way of Aaron's progress at various points during his ongoing development. Every time I got on the phone, the experience was always different and the outcome was more positive. My wife is convinced that a male voice commands a different type of feedback and response than female voice gets under normal circumstances

Fathers can be very influential especially in situations where our involvement demands a straight answer like "right now." Leveraging this kind of influence is definitely a no-nonsense approach that can have a profound effect on your ability as a family to get things done fast and moving in the right direction.

This approach has worked for our family on numerous occasions when an urgent event needed to happen and we were getting the run-around, to put it mildly. I've noticed after doing this a couple of times that the overall conversation takes a different tone when I am on the phone or face-to-face driving outcomes and results for the benefit of my child. On many occasions my wife has assigned me as the "cleanup" guy when she was having multiple challenges just getting answers to basic questions.

Our strategy is really simple: my wife initiates, and I come in at the middle or end to reinforce our position. This is definitely not the perfect solution because we are not always at the same place at the same time and there is a lag between the initial discussion and a follow-up conversation by me. Sometimes I have to do the follow-up on the phone as opposed to face to face which is my preference. However this does drive towards better overall outcomes. We do still run into the occasional challenges and hurdles, but they are very mild compared to what we had to deal with when we had no strategy to get past the roadblocks. Now we are more confident in our approach, and we always prevail in the end. Frustration is not the enemy, but a friend!

When fathers participate and are very visible as advocates, things get done without the emotions coming into play. It was important for me to spare my wife the frustration that comes with being ignored or given the run-around by those who are supposed to be helping.

Now, a lot gets done over a shorter period of time. Don't ask me how and why, it's just is the way it happens to unfold! The approach is simple; there is nothing to lose but everything to gain in the effort. The entire landscape changes because fathers are naturally "hard core" and straight to the point.

Let's be honest: most of the organizations that serve and support our children are very familiar with dealing with the mothers on a regular basis. Mothers can become worn down, very sensitive, and emotional for good reasons over time, especially when things are not happening as anticipated and there is a lot of resistance against their efforts. Just recently I heard another mother say, "I can't do this anymore; I am tired and frustrated!"

It's not good for mother or child when it gets to that point. Let's face it: we all are so busy and have good reasons to relax and staunch this constant outpouring of energy. However, the point is that more needs to be done to share the load if at all possible. I speak from experience. Why is that? Fathers are in short supply when it comes to all-out advocacy for their children with autism. When the fathers attend at a meeting or conference, they are taken very seriously by teachers, therapists, doctors, and other parents. Initially most fathers, I myself being one of those, "once upon a time" believed that I could not influence change, so why bother! But fathers really do have the power and influence to become stronger advocates for their children. Believe me, I know better now: Yes, I can, and yes, I will make a difference.

Normally, my conversation starts with this question: What do we need to do to move this forward? This is a no-nonsense approach that is not rude or intrusive but rather results oriented. When it comes to leading the charge for my son, it is very important for me to carve out the time for programs including special education and information-centered community fairs, symposiums, and other events that provide education and support for the special-needs community. I only have one chance to get it right. I normally lead the male charge by default at school PTA and town hall meetings, or whenever there is a program available from which I could learn something new about existing and developing services to support my son. This is the essence of advocacy. I cannot be at all the meetings all the time, but I have committed to attend more times than not. Believe me, these are the times I have really learned a lot of tips that turned into action items. It's been an education from which I draw intelligence to become more effective in my role as an advocate.

The worst experience that ever happened to me was an emergency situation in which my wife was the only adult member of the family who could answer those subtle finer questions about our son's medical history. Getting caught off-guard can happen when you least expect it, especially when it's imperative to know the answers.

My wife was not always available to bail me out of that doctor's visit, so I fumbled on basic questions that I should have known the answers to. It was so embarrassing when I could not respond to a question like "what is the dosage?" My immediate response was "I will get that information back to you shortly!" It worked in a pinch, but it was not good enough. I had this doctor give me the stare and it was so obvious what he was actually thinking. Lesson learned: be prepared and be informed. This is why I stay current as an advocate, even during times when I really don't have a lot of time to dedicate to it. It's not possible for me to be at all the doctor's appointments and therapy visits, so my wife and I go through a debriefing exercise with all the "need-to-know" information. She is very good at keeping me informed and current.

Not having all the information was a wake-up call for me. It was a real prompt for me to be in the know going forward. It is a very uncomfortable place for a father to be in, especially when absence is not intentional. I get these unintended strange looks that gently insinuate "where have you been?" So I stay informed and connected, and advocate at every opportunity that arises. I have discovered that the experience on this journey becomes easier and much more pleasant for the entire family, and is less stressful overall.

Advocacy has helped us achieve our goals and the expected outcomes we have set for our son. It's much easier when great minds come together to figure it out!

Now, my wife and I can spend the rest of our available combined time to focus on getting the best services and support possible for Aaron's welfare and development. Advocacy has helped us learn how to navigate the bureaucracy of social services, its systematic slow pace, and the unending mountain of paperwork and roadblocks. Advocacy has been very effective at helping us move things along expeditiously. Sometimes it requires getting annoyed with the system to remove the "logjam" and get things moving along.

Through advocacy we were introduced to the Katie Beckett waiver by a parent in the network as a way to get additional services fully paid through Medicaid. The requirements for this program are not based on family income. Historically we paid for everything else that the insurance would not cover. Because there is a nonnegotiable set of income-related restrictions attached to other government-funded programs, we were never approved for Medicaid benefits for Aaron. This prevented us from being accepted after multiple applications and pursuits. On the first application we were denied.

Lesson leaned! We had to find someone who understood the Katie Becket process thoroughly. We found a paid resource that was able to gather all the details, and we were accepted on the second try. The only downside is that an application has to be refilled annually, but families can do the re-file by themselves without having to pay another fee each year. Just copy the previous paperwork that was accepted and add any current information to strengthen your child's need for eligibility and ongoing services. It's that simple.

It got to the point where I needed to be the voice for our child, especially dealing with city and county school systems. My wife and I spent an enormous amount of hours understanding our rights and entitlement for a special-needs child in the school system. I discovered very quickly that there are good and bad experiences when dealing with local authorities and board of education school systems. It was easy to see in some schools that there was a lack of interest and care for children with autism. I soon found out that if I did not care passionately enough to put in the extra time and effort for my son, then there was no way I could expect the school to be the surrogate backstop. So, my advice to myself is to always be the number-one advocate, no matter what my schedule looks like. Time is of the essence when dealing with local authorities in pursuit for services. It's challenging now more than ever, as budget cuts and cost restrictions become the excuse for lack of available funding.

Be an active advocate, or see your child fall into this black hole, only to be sent on a "fast track" called pre-kindergarten through twelfth grade, which leads our children with autism to nowhere. It is important to be very specific about the severity of your child's needs. In the past, support services we requested were continuously shot down. Teachers and administrators said no budget dollars were allocated; therefore our requests could not be accommodated.

We were offered less-than-satisfactory alternatives as taxpayers. So, we forced their hand to make better accommodations. If we couldn't get what we were expecting in school district A, we suggested school district B and demanded that the school district pick up the tab for the transportation to another school district. The end result was that they came up with a better alternative.

Later on, we recognized the good traits of school A, but A was not meeting our son's short-term needs, so he fell short on long-term goals. There was a very unfortunate incident we experienced in the elementary school system. So, we pushed and asked the middle school to take him on earlier than normal. He was challenged at first, and being in middle school was a stretch goal, but eventually it worked out perfectly for him!

The process of advocacy is a lifelong endeavor, so it is easier when you double up with other parents or community networks. Numbers really do work in this instance. Never get caught in the "shame trap" or feel pressured about stepping up or worried about being seen as a nuisance. I've been at different venues where parents have been open about what they are personally dealing with. They draw strength from other parents. Believe me; it's very refreshing to know we are not alone.

When parents share like experiences from a variety of circumstances and experiences, it speaks volumes. I have picked up a lot of good information and resources that have enabled me as a parent to do battle with schools and local government agencies. Advocacy is a worthwhile and rewarding investment of time. I know what I'm talking about. I have been in many meetings where I was the only male advocating!

Advocacy takes a lot of time and sacrificial effort. My personal time on the computer, on the phone, and knocking on doors is unending. Advocacy has a permanent spot on my calendar with all the other roles and responsibilities that I have at home, work, and at church.

At first glance advocacy is hard work. But as you get yourself into a consistent routine, things seem to fit in together like a puzzle. Advocacy helped me to re-channel my energy and focus. I was trying to do everything on my own and really did not accomplish much. It was very helpful to take time off from work to do a lot of the running around during work hours. Working for a company that offers flexibility to do this makes a huge difference. I have known parents to turn to Grandparents or close friends to help out when it was not always convenient or possible to do some necessary information gathering or making appointments during working hours. Whenever possible if Saturdays were an option for covering tasks like meeting with a non-profit church group to discuss respite care, or a summer camp opportunity this would be my first option.

Advocacy for me has been a special project requiring my full attention. I make it happen for Aaron every day. "Busy" and "tired" are not deterrents or words that I use in my vocabulary. I always remember that there is a very small window of time to make the most impact in my son's life.

CHAPTER 11

TOUGH LOVE

hoosing between using kid gloves with our child with autism or invoking tough love may have been one of the hardest and most productive decisions my wife and I have had to make. We both had differing opinions on what was needed to get Aaron to a place that he could become very independent, having an opinion for himself and being the best that he could be as a child and later as an adult. If Aaron was required to clean his room and do the laundry it would have to be done and he could come to me and get one response and to his mother and get another. We have to send the same message.

Nothing is worse than sending mixed messages. Aaron would have homework that he needed to finish at home. Sometimes the exercise went beyond his bedtime because it took a little longer for him to understand the concept. We both had to be willing to get the work done

in preparation for the next day. He would end up going to bed later than usual and still had to get up early in the morning.

This is where the rubber meets the road in relationships. My wife thought I was a bit harsh with my methods and I agree. Looking ahead it was either invoking the harsh reality that being autistic will not be an acceptable excuse in the workplace if he cannot stay on task, get an assignment done and be on time. That is the long-term reality of raising a child with autism that may be able to work independently in the community and be his or her own person. This is the aspiration of every parent that I know has a child with autism.

The more thought I put into it, the more it became apparent that when our son independently moves out on his own, he will need to be prepared for a world that is a not a friendly place, a world that does not have patience for those kids and adults with challenges they are still working hard to overcome.

My concept is simple, how can I help Aaron function in the broader community. What happens if my wife and I are not around, then what? Getting to that point is a rocky and painful journey. I was willing to be very practical with Aaron to instill the discipline that was a minimum requirement to function in different social and employment settings. He was not allowed to wonder off from a task. He starts and he finishes. That is the rule. He struggled, and sometimes the feeling was probably this is not going to work, so why put all the

pressure on him to do his work, clean up after himself, be responsible.

We had to use common sense when looking at Aarons ability to be responsible. This meant looking past the autism and just seeing Aaron for who he is. A child that will one day become an adult and may have responsibility placed on him. Even if he goes to a group home setting one of the requirements is that he has to be self sufficient. Long term he may go to a training institution. The requirements are the same; he has to be self-sufficient with very little supervision. These capabilities do not come naturally for Aaron. They have to be learned. The only way to learn it is to have it reinforced. We never use autism as an excuse for Aaron not to be socially responsible. If he misbehaves he knows that there are consequences. As a father I had to do what I had to do in the spirit of love. I have been tough and sometimes my wife had to come back and smooth it over.

Aaron is reasonably responsible and takes ownership for his actions. Not doing everything for him, and treating him like a baby was the best thing we could have done. It has helped his productivity. Aaron is very resourceful and always wants to help. Aaron can stay at overnight camps and days away from home and we do not have to worry how he is coping.

Had we not invoked tough love nothing would have changed. We would deny Aaron the opportunity to help

himself in any given situation without having to entirely depend on anyone else.

There have been too many examples that I have seen along the way with parents going either way. They ended up having different approaches to the same issue. In the process they sent mixed messages to the child and pulling themselves apart in the process. Our experience is that it is important to be on the same page first, then stick to the plan, no matter how uncomfortable the process might be. The agreed approach needs to be consistent to get the best outcome.

Aaron's condition was driving his behavior, or lack of it, and most of the time it was out of his control. Making excuses for the behavior "just because of his condition" was not going to cut it for us. We would be doing him and ourselves a great disservice by just doing the minimum to get by.

There have been many lessons we've learned along the way with respect to making tough choices when our more sensitive side would just have had us leave it alone. I learned a long time ago that if a plant is left alone, the weeds and other elements will prevent it from reaching its peak.

One of my personal angst is procrastination especially when so many demands are on my time. Tough love is not for tomorrow but for right now! I would often say to myself when I get tired or overwhelmed, "We can do this tomorrow." But tomorrow becomes next week, and then rolls into next month and perhaps next year. The

symptom of a weak start in the evaluation process is always procrastination. Pushing myself to take action right now has helped me psychologically on multiple occasions! You get what you take action on, not what you expect!

In the period after Aaron was diagnosed, denial set in, and I wasted a lot of time believing and hoping that autism would just go away. With that in mind, the change I was expecting never materialized. My experience has been to take command and earnestly pursue testing, and to find a team of specialists to evaluate your child at the earliest point "of autism awareness."

Procrastination is the biggest hurdle in working to get the best care and resources for your child because it is self-imposed, impractical, and prolongs the problem without relief or solution. I am now more sensitive to the need to be vigilant, even when I do not know how and where to start. Abdicating my responsibility is a thing of the past. I have put all these mistakes down to a learning experience. Addressing autism is a practical matter. Once I got started and figured out what needed to be done in short order, I just went with my instinct and did it without trying to predict the end.

Lost time and a good opportunity cannot be reclaimed or recaptured. Sometimes it is necessary to have someone close enough to kick the tires or provide additional prompting to keep pushing forward pass the finish line. For me, my wife's lead and prompting have really helped tremendously.

Looking back I wouldn't do anything differently because the mistakes were how I learned successful strategies. We worked with what we had, and it worked out. No two fathers in the same situation need to face the same challenge twice when books like this are available and filled with resources, tips, learning experiences, and good information that is honest and informative.

We cannot change the past, but we can impact and change the present. For instance, my wife started out carrying the weight of running around and doing a lot of the coordination. Now the load is shared.

Don't leave it up to the mothers. Get involved. Once you get used to it and develop a routine as the progress unfolds, the experience becomes very fulfilling and rewarding for the entire family. What started out as a bad experience does not have to continue or end that way; it's all about rising to the challenge. Did I feel sometimes that I was in over my head? Absolutely! Putting it all into perspective, I made the best decisions in each moment, and I can live with that.

I am confident that my son will reach his potential and be closer to his dreams, goals, and desires for a rewarding and enriched life. Never say no to the inconvenience of extending a little further, and never give up on making progress in the face of adversity.

Looking back, on all we have done we have seen contrastingly progressive results over time. We eventually realized that everything we know about autism and how to manage it is a learn as you go process

being developed and understood one day at a time, one challenge at a time.

This is a familiar discussion that I have had the pleasure of engaging fathers on in waiting rooms or connecting at a ball game. This book will serve as a reminder for some fathers; for others I hope it will provide needed insight and hope during the challenging times. At the end of the day, we all have one common goal: to do the best, whatever it takes, for our child even if it means invoking tough love.

CHAPTER 12:

THE FINANCIAL
IMPACT OF AUTISM

F amilies of various income levels are feeling the financial strain. Many health insurance policies do not cover autism treatments, while those that do often have severe limits and restrictions. Apparently there is diminishing government and private financial assistance available as a result of shrinking budgets and service reductions. In many cases these children will need assistance all their lives. Making sure there is money for the future is something else parents worry about.

Parents can often end up paying for many of their treatments from their own income and savings. In the early years, autism coverage under health insurance can be denied multiple times before approval. But claims for certain therapies, tests, and treatments are often denied.

I was very aggressive about appealing those denials, and I often won. But even with good coverage, I needed to pay enormous amounts out of pocket to come close to giving my son the forty to sixty hours of behavioral, occupational, and physical therapies including speech and language each year that were the recommended minimum visits.

A diagnosis of autism affects the entire family, emotionally, spiritually, and financially, but autism does not have to be an expensive endeavor if you have awareness of the available programs and support services. Parents and caregivers of children with autism do have options.

I use all the free services and resources I can find in conjunction with my medical insurance coverage first. Then I pay out of pocket as the last resort.

Eventually I was able to obtain financial assistance for Aaron through a special part of the Medicaid program called the Katie Becket Waiver. I would recommend that parents of a child with special needs apply for this waiver because it is not income dependent. The form is available online. Complete the form with supporting medical records, bank details and other relevant information and then take to your local Department of Social Services. A case manager will be assigned. The case manger reviews your case to make sure it is complete, the package is sent off to a medical review board for approval.

Medicaid has come up with creative ways to deliver

health care services around the country for children with special needs. Medicaid.Gov provides a wealth of services information on every available waiver by state by program. States have now expanded coverage for children. Children of families with very high incomes can qualify for the Children Health Care Insurance Program (CHIP). CHIP funding has been extended through 2015. Parents can plan for their Childs health care needs using this program. With extensive cuts in services at the State and Federal level. This is good information to have.

Comp Now or comprehensive support waivers provide a wide range of support services like respite care, specialized medical equipment and supplies vehicle adaptation and behavioral supports to name a couple of examples.

Treatment for a special needs child is extremely expensive. Direct medical and nonmedical costs can add up to as much as $72,000 a year for a child with an extreme case of the disorder, and even $67,000 a year for those on the lower end of the spectrum.

This figure includes doctor visits, prescription drugs, occupational and speech therapy, and expenses for things like special education support, camps and childcare, travel, and food. "It can cost $3.2 million to take care of an autistic person over the course of his or her lifetime.

More families today having to deal with the current economic woes are grappling with the disorder more than ever before. Autism is the fastest-growing developmental disorder on record, occurring today in one out of eighty-eight children. Four out of five are boys. Statistics suggest that autism is growing at a rate of 10 percent to 17 percent per year. At this rate, there will be over four million Americans affected in the next decade.

One of every 110 eight-year-old children in the United States alone has been diagnosed with autism—and one out of every seventy boys, according to the latest survey. Combine these numbers with statistics out of Canada, Latin America, Europe, and Asia, and we are looking at disturbing development impacting children, families, and communities. Dealing with the fallout from the financial meltdown is just another strain on families of children with autism.

Although direct financial support may be limited and hard to obtain, there are several autism information and advocacy groups that routinely help parents navigate financial hurdles. Here is a road map parents can use to get started.

CHECK YOUR INSURANCE

Coverage for specialized autism treatments is still far from common, but it is improving. Some large employers offer policies that cover treatment, and thirty-four states have passed laws mandating at least some autism-related coverage. The Autism Society's Web site lists these states. New states are also coming online in support of this specific piece of legislation to mandate coverage for its autistic population.

Alabama

Requires a health benefit plan to provide coverage for the screening, diagnosis and treatment of autism spectrum disorder for individuals age nine or under in policies and contracts to employers with at least 51 employees for at least 50 percent of its working days for the preceding calendar year. Coverage is limited to treatment that is prescribed by the insured's licensed physician or licensed psychologist and includes: behavioral health treatment, pharmacy care, psychiatric care, psychological care, and therapeutic care (which includes services provided by a licensed and certified speech therapist).

Citation: Ala. Code §10A-20-6.16 and 27-21A-23

Alaska

Requires insurers provide coverage for the diagnosis and treatment of autism spectrum disorder for individuals under 21 effective January 1, 2013. Covered treatment includes medically necessary pharmacy care, psychiatric care, psychological care, habilitative or rehabilitative care, and therapeutic care (which include services provided by a licensed speech-language pathologist.) There is no limit on the number of visits an individual may make to an autism services provider.

Citation: Alaska Stat. §21.42.397

Arizona

Requires policies issued by certain health insurers to provide coverage for the diagnosis and treatment of autism spectrum disorder. Treatment includes: diagnosis, assessment and services.

Note: Speech language services are not clearly defined in the statue. However, behavioral therapy is specifically defined as applied behavioral analysis and coverage limitations for behavioral therapy are set out.

Citation: Ariz. Rev. Stat. Ann. §20-826.04; §20-1057.11; §20-1402.03; §20-1404.03

Arkansas

Requires health benefit plans issues or renewed on or after October 1, 2011 to provide for coverage for the diagnosis and treatment of autism spectrum disorder. Treatment includes: (i) Applied behavior analysis when provided by or supervised by a Board Certified Behavior Analyst; (ii) Pharmacy care; (iii) Psychiatric care; (iv) Psychological care; (v) Therapeutic care (which includes services provided by licensed speech therapists, occupational therapists, or physical therapists); and (vi) Equipment determined necessary to provide evidence-based treatment; provided such treatments determined by a licensed physician to be medically necessary and evidence-based.

Citation: Ark. Code Ann. §23-99-418

California

Requires health care service plan contract provide hospital, medical, or surgical coverage to provide coverage for behavioral health treatment for pervasive developmental disorder or autism no later than July 1, 2012. Treatments include: professional services and treatment programs, including applied behavior analysis and evidence-based behavior intervention programs that develop or restore, to the maximum extent practicable, the functioning of an individual with pervasive developmental disorder or autism and includes speech-language pathology and audiology.

Citation: Cal. Health & Safety Code §1374.73

Colorado

Requires all health benefit plans issued or renewed after July 1, 2010 to provide coverage for the assessment, diagnosis, and treatment of autism spectrum disorders for a child. Treatments include: evaluation and assessment services; Behavior training and behavior management and applied behavior analysis; habilitative or rehabilitative care, including, but not limited to, occupational therapy, physical therapy, or speech therapy, or any combination of those therapies; pharmacy care and medication; psychiatric care; psychological care; and therapeutic care, including, but is not limited to, speech, occupational, and applied behavior analytic and physical therapies.

Citation: Colo. Rev. Stat. §10-16-104

Connecticut

Requires that each group health insurance policy to provide coverage for the diagnosis and treatment of autism spectrum disorders. Treatments include: behavioral therapy; prescription drugs; direct psychiatric or consultative services provided by a licensed psychiatrist; direct psychological or consultative services provided by a licensed psychologist; physical therapy provided by a licensed physical therapist; speech and language pathology services provided by a licensed speech and language pathologist; and occupational therapy provided by a licensed occupational therapist, provided such treatments are (1) medically necessary, and (2) identified and ordered by a licensed physician, licensed psychologist or licensed clinical social worker for an insured who is diagnosed with an autism spectrum disorder.

Citation: Conn. Gen. Stat. §38a-514b (as amended by S.B. 301 (2009)

Delaware

Requires all health benefit plans to provide coverage for the screening and diagnosis of autism spectrum disorders and the treatment of autism spectrum disorders in individuals less than 21 years of age. Treatment includes: behavioral health treatment; pharmacy care; psychiatric care; psychological care; therapeutic care (including services provided by a speech, occupational, or physical therapists or an aide or assistant under their supervision); items and equipment necessary to provide, receive, or advance in the above listed services, including those necessary for applied behavioral analysis; and any care for individuals with autism spectrum disorders that is determined by the Secretary of the Department of Health and Social Services, based upon their review of best practices and/or evidence-based research, to be medically necessary.

Coverage under this section shall not be denied on the basis that the treatment is habilitative or no restorative in nature.

Citation: Del. Code Ann. tit. 18, §3361

Florida

Requires health insurance plans to provide coverage to an eligible individual for:

1. Well-baby and well-child screening for diagnosing the presence of autism spectrum disorder.

2. Treatment of autism spectrum disorder through speech therapy, occupational therapy, physical therapy, and applied behavior analysis.

Coverage for the services shall be limited to $36,000 annually and may not exceed $200,000 in total lifetime benefits for an individual under 18 years of age or an individual 18 years of age or older who is in high school who has been diagnosed as having a developmental disability at 8 years of age or younger.

Citation: Fla. Stat. Ann. §627.6686

Illinois

Requires certain health insurers to provide individuals under 21 years of age coverage for the diagnosis of autism spectrum disorders and for the treatment of autism spectrum disorders. Treatment includes the following care prescribed, provided, or ordered for an individual diagnosed with an autism spectrum disorder by (A) a physician licensed to practice medicine in all its branches, or (B) a certified, registered, or licensed health care professional with expertise in treating effects of autism spectrum disorders when the care is determined to be medically necessary and ordered by a physician licensed to practice medicine in all its branches; psychiatric care, meaning direct, consultative, or diagnostic services provided by a licensed psychiatrist; psychological care, meaning direct or consultative services provided by a licensed psychologist; habilitative or rehabilitative care, meaning professional, counseling, and guidance services and treatment programs, including applied behavior analysis, that are intended to develop, maintain, and restore the functioning of an individual; therapeutic care, including behavioral, speech, occupational, and physical therapies. Coverage provided shall be subject to a maximum benefit of $36,000 per year, but shall not be subject to any limits on the number of visits to a service provider.

Citation: Ill. Comp. Stat. ch. 215, § 5/356z.14

Indiana

Requires that group and individual policies to provide coverage for the treatment of a pervasive developmental disorder of an insured. A pervasive developmental disorder is defined as a neurological condition, including Asperger's syndrome and autism, as defined in the most recent edition of the Diagnostic and Statistical Manual of Mental Disorders of the American Psychiatric Association. The coverage required may not be subject to dollar limits, deductibles, or coinsurance provisions that are less favorable to an insured than the dollar limits, deductibles, or coinsurance provisions that apply to physical illness generally under the accident and sickness insurance policy.

Note: Speech language services are not specifically defined in the statute. Coverage is "limited to treatment that is prescribed by the insured's treating physician in accordance with a treatment plan."

Citation: Ind. Code Ann. §27-8-14.2; §27-13-7-14.7

Iowa

Requires a group plan established for employees of the state providing for third-party payment or prepayment of health, medical, and surgical coverage benefits shall provide coverage benefits to covered individuals less than twenty-one years of age for the diagnostic assessment of autism spectrum disorders and for the treatment of autism spectrum disorders. Treatment includes medically necessary pharmacy care, psychiatric care, psychological care, rehabilitative care, and therapeutic care (including services provided by a licensed speech pathologist, licensed occupational therapist, or licensed physical therapist). Coverage shall not exceed thirty-six thousand dollars per year but shall not be subject to any limits on the number of visits to an autism service provider for treatment of autism spectrum disorders.

Citation: Iowa Code §514C.28

Kansas

Requires that the state employees' health care commission to provide for the coverage of services for the diagnosis and treatment of autism spectrum disorder in any covered individual whose age is less than 19 years, effective January 1, 2011. Coverage is determined in consultation with the autism services provider and the patient. Coverage for benefits for any covered person diagnosed with one or more autism spectrum disorders and whose age is between birth and less than seven years shall not exceed $36,000 per year. Coverage for benefits for any covered person diagnosed with one or more autism spectrum disorders and whose age is at least seven years and less than 19 years shall not exceed $27,000 per year.

Note: Speech language services are not clearly defined in the statue. However, behavioral therapy is specifically defined as applied behavioral analysis and coverage limitations for behavioral therapy are set out.

Citation: Kan. Stat. Ann. §75-6524

Kentucky

Requires large group health benefit plan and individual and small group market health benefit plans provide coverage for the diagnosis and treatment of autism spectrum disorders.

Large group health benefit plan

Treatment includes: medical care; habilitative or rehabilitative care; pharmacy care, if covered by the plan; psychiatric care; psychological care; therapeutic care (includes services provided by licensed speech therapists, occupational therapists, or physical therapists); and applied behavior analysis prescribed or ordered by a licensed health or allied health professional. Coverage under this section shall be subject to a maximum annual benefit per covered individual as follows: for individuals between the ages of one (1) through their seventh birthday, the maximum annual benefit shall be $50,000 per individual; for individuals between the ages of seven (7) through 21, the maximum benefit shall be $1,000, per month per individual.

**Individual and small group
market health benefit plan**

All health benefit plans in the individual and small group market shall provide coverage for pharmacy care, if covered by the plan: psychiatric care; psychological care; therapeutic care (includes services provided by licensed speech therapists, occupational therapists, or physical therapists); applied behavior analysis; habilitative and rehabilitative care. Coverage for autism spectrum disorders shall be subject to $1,000 maximum benefit per month, per covered individual.

Citation: Ky. Rev. Stat. §304.17A-142 [PDF], 304.17A-143

Louisiana

Requires health coverage plans to provide coverage for the diagnosis and treatment of autism spectrum disorders in individuals less than 21 years of age. Treatment includes: habilitative or rehabilitative care; pharmacy care; psychiatric care; psychological care; therapeutic care (including services provided by licensed or certified speech therapists, occupational therapists, or physical therapists licensed or certified in this state), provided the care prescribed, provided, or ordered for an individual diagnosed with one of the autism spectrum disorders by a physician or psychologist who shall be licensed in this state and who shall supervise provision of such care. Coverage shall be subject to a maximum benefit of $36,000 per year and a lifetime maximum benefit of $144,000. There shall not be any limits on the number of visits an individual may make to an autism services provider.

Citation: La. Rev. Stat. Ann. §22-1050

Maine

Requires all individual and group health insurance policies and contracts must provide coverage for autism spectrum disorders for an individual covered under a policy or contract who is 5 years of age or under in accordance with the following. Treatment includes: habilitative or rehabilitative services, including applied behavior analysis or other professional or counseling services; counseling services provided by a licensed psychiatrist, psychologist, clinical professional counselor or clinical social worker; and therapy services provided by a licensed or certified speech therapist, occupational therapist or physical therapist.

Citation: Me. Rev. Stat. Ann. tit. 24A §2768; 24A §2847-T; 24A §4259

Massachusetts

Effective January 1, 2011, requires insurance coverage for autism. Treatment includes the following care prescribed, provided or ordered for an individual diagnosed with 1 of the autism spectrum disorders by a licensed physician or a licensed psychologist who determines the care to be medically necessary: habilitative or rehabilitative care; pharmacy care; psychiatric care; psychological care; and therapeutic care, including speech therapy services. Certain insurers may be exempt from requirements for 3 years.

Citation: Mass. Gen. Laws. ch. 32A §25; ch. 175 §47AA; ch. 176A §8DD ch. 176B §4DD; ch. 176G §4V

Michigan

Effective January 1, 2014, requires a health care corporation group or no group certificate to provide coverage for the diagnosis of autism spectrum disorders and treatment of autism spectrum disorders. Treatment of autism spectrum disorders prescribed or ordered for an individual diagnosed with 1 of the autism spectrum disorders by a licensed physician or a licensed psychologist includes: (i) Behavioral health treatment; (ii) Pharmacy care; (iii) Psychiatric care; (iv) Psychological care; and (v) Therapeutic care (including services provided by a licensed or certified speech therapist, occupational therapist, physical therapist, or social worker.) Coverage for treatment of autism spectrum disorders may be limited to a member through 18 years of age and may be subject to a maximum annual benefit as follows: (i) For a covered member through 6 years of age, $50,000.00; (ii) For a covered member from 7 years of age through 12 years of age, $40,000.00; and (iii) For a covered member from 13 years of age through 18 years of age, $30,000.00.

Citation: Mich. Comp. Laws §550.1461(e) as added by S.B. 414; S.B. 415; S.B. 981

Missouri

Requires all group health benefit plans that are delivered, issued for delivery, continued, or renewed on or after January 1, 2011, to provide coverage for the diagnosis and treatment of autism spectrum disorders to the extent that such diagnosis and treatment is not already covered by the health benefit plan. Treatment for autism spectrum disorders, care prescribed or ordered for an individual diagnosed with an autism spectrum disorder by a licensed physician or licensed psychologist, include: psychiatric care; psychological care; habilitative or rehabilitative care, including applied behavior analysis therapy; therapeutic care (including services provided by licensed speech therapists, occupational therapists, or physical therapists); and pharmacy care.

Citation: Mo. Rev. Stat. §376.1224

Montana

Requires each group disability policy, certificate of insurance, or membership contract that is delivered, issued for delivery, renewed, extended, or modified in this state must provide coverage for diagnosis and treatment of autism spectrum disorders for a covered child 18 years of age or younger. Treatment includes: habilitative or rehabilitative care that is prescribed, provided, or ordered by a licensed physician or licensed psychologist, including but not limited to professional, counseling, and guidance services and treatment programs that are medically necessary to develop and restore, to the maximum extent practicable, the functioning of the covered child; medications prescribed by a physician; psychiatric or psychological care; and therapeutic care that is provided by a speech-language pathologist, audiologist, occupational therapist, or physical therapist licensed in this state. Coverage for treatment of autism spectrum disorders under this section may be limited to a maximum benefit of:

- $50,000 a year for a child 8 years of age or younger; and
- $20,000 a year for a child 9 years of age through 18 years of age

Citation: Mont. Code Ann. §33-22-515

Nevada

Effective January 1, 2011—Requires that an individual health benefit plan to provide an option of coverage for screening for and diagnosis of autism spectrum disorders and for treatment of autism spectrum disorders for persons covered by the policy under the age of 18 or, if enrolled in high school, until the person reaches the age of 22. Treatment of autism spectrum disorders must be identified in a treatment plan and may include medically necessary habilitative or rehabilitative care, prescription care, psychiatric care, psychological care, behavior therapy or therapeutic care (including services provided by licensed or certified speech pathologists, occupational therapists and physical therapists).

Citation: Ne. Rev. Stat. §689A.0435

New Hampshire

Requires insurance coverage for diagnosis and treatment of pervasive developmental disorder or autism for all group policies, contracts, and certificates issued or renewed on or after January 1, 2011. Treatment includes: professional services and treatment programs, including applied behavioral analysis; prescribed pharmaceuticals subject to the same terms and conditions of the policy as other prescribed pharmaceuticals; direct or consultative services provided by a licensed professional including a licensed psychiatrist, licensed advanced practice registered nurse, licensed psychologist, or licensed clinical social worker; and Services provided by a licensed speech therapist, licensed occupational therapist, or licensed physical therapist.

Citation: N.H. Rev. Stat. Ann. §417-E:2

New Jersey
Requires specified health insurance policies and health benefit plans to provide benefits for treatment of autism or other developmental disability. Coverage shall include: medically necessary occupational therapy, physical therapy, and speech therapy, as prescribed through a treatment plan. The maximum benefit amount for a covered person in any calendar year through 2012 shall be $37,080.

Citation: N.J. Rev. Stat. §17:48-6ii; §17:48A-7ff; 17B:26-2.1cc; 17B:27-46.1ii; 17B:27A-7.16; 17B:27A-19.20; §26-2J-4.34; §52:14-17.29p; 52:14-17.46.6b

New Mexico
Requires specified health insurance policy, health care plan or certificate of health insurance shall provide coverage to an eligible individual who is nineteen

139

years of age or younger, or an eligible individual who is twenty-two years of age or younger and is enrolled in high school, for:

1. Well-baby and well-child screening for diagnosing the presence of autism spectrum disorder; and

2. Treatment of autism spectrum disorder through speech therapy, occupational therapy, physical therapy and applied behavioral analysis.

Coverage shall be limited to $36,000 annually and shall not exceed $200,000 in total lifetime benefits.

Citation: N.M. Stat. Ann §59A-22-49; §59A-23-7.9; §59A-46-50; §59A-47-45

New York

Require physician services, major medical or similar comprehensive-type coverage to provide coverage for the screening, diagnosis and treatment of autism spectrum disorder. Coverage includes, therapeutic care, which is habilitative or no restorative, provided by a licensed or certified speech therapist.

Citation: N.Y. Isc Law §3216

Oregon

Requires health benefit plans to cover for a child enrolled in the plan who is under 18 years of age and who has been diagnosed with a pervasive developmental disorder (including autism) all medical services, including rehabilitation services, that are medically necessary and are otherwise covered under the plan. Rehabilitation services are defined as physical therapy, occupational therapy or speech therapy services to restore or improve function.

Citation: Or. Rev. Stat. §743A.190

Note: 743A.190 was added to and made a part of the Insurance Code by legislative action but was not added to ORS chapter 743A or any series therein.

Pennsylvania
Require health insurance policy or government program to provide coverage for individuals less than 21 years of age for the diagnostic assessment and treatment of autism spectrum disorder. Treatment includes: pharmacy care, psychiatric care, psychological care, rehabilitative care and therapeutic care (includes services provided by speech language pathologists, occupational therapists or physical therapists) that is medically necessary and prescribed, ordered or provided by a licensed physician, licensed physician assistant, licensed psychologist, licensed clinical social worker or certified registered nurse practitioner. Coverage provided under this section by an insurer shall be subject to a maximum benefit of $37,080 per year and is subject to any limits on the number of visits to an autism service provider for treatment of autism spectrum disorders.
Citation: Pa. Cons. Stat. tit. 40 §764h

Rhode Island

Requires every group health insurance contract, or every group hospital or medical expense insurance policy, or group policy delivered, issued for delivery, or renewed in this state, by any health insurance carrier, on or after January 1, 2012, to provide coverage for autism spectrum disorders. These provisions are not subject to the Small Employer Health Insurance Availability Act, or the Individual Health Insurance Coverage Act. Benefits include coverage for applied behavior analysis, physical therapy, and speech therapy and occupational therapy services for the treatment of Autism spectrum disorders. The benefits will continue until the covered individual reaches the age of fifteen.

Citation: R.I. Gen. Laws §20.11

South Carolina

Require that health insurance plan to provide coverage for the treatment of autism spectrum disorder. To be eligible for benefits and coverage, an individual must be diagnosed with autistic spectrum disorder at age eight or younger. The benefits and coverage provided must be provided to any eligible person under sixteen years of age.

Note: Speech language services are not specifically defined in the statute. Coverage is "limited to treatment that is prescribed by the insured's treating medical doctor in accordance with a treatment plan." Although behavioral therapy is not specifically defined, the statute does set out a cap of $50,000 per year for coverage of behavioral therapy.

Citation: S.C. Code Ann. §38-71-280

Texas

Requires a health benefit plan to provide coverage to an enrollee who is diagnosed with autism spectrum disorder from the date of diagnosis until the enrollee completes nine years of age. If an enrollee who is being treated for autism spectrum disorder becomes 10 years of age or older and continues to need treatment, this does not preclude coverage of treatment and services. Treatment may include services such as: evaluation and assessment services; applied behavior analysis; behavior training and behavior management; speech therapy; occupational therapy; physical therapy; or medications or nutritional supplements used to address symptoms of autism spectrum disorder.

Citation: Tex. Ins. Code Ann. §1355.015

Vermont

Requires a health insurance plan to provide coverage for the diagnosis and treatment of autism spectrum disorders, including applied behavior analysis supervised by a nationally board-certified behavior analyst, for children, beginning at 18 months of age and continuing until the child reaches age six or enters the first grade, whichever occurs first. Treatment includes:

habilitative or rehabilitative care; pharmacy care; psychiatric care; psychological care; and therapeutic care (includes services provided by licensed or certified speech language pathologists, occupational therapists, physical therapists, or social workers), if the physician or psychologist determines the care to be medically necessary. The provisions go into effect on or after July 1, 2011, on such date as a health insurer offers, issues, or renews the health insurance plan, but in no event later than July 1, 2012.

Citation: Vt. Code Ann. tit. 8 § 4088i

Virginia

Requires health insurance plans issued or renewed after January 1, 2012, to provide coverage for the diagnosis and the treatment of autism spectrum disorder in individuals from age two through age six. An individual who is being treated and continues to need treatment for autism spectrum disorder and becomes seven years of age or older is not precluded from coverage of treatment and services. Treatment shall be determined by a licensed physician or a licensed psychologist to be medically necessary, and includes: (i) behavioral health treatment, (ii) pharmacy care, (iii) psychiatric care, (iv) psychological care, (v) therapeutic care (which includes services provided by licensed or certified speech therapists, occupational therapists, physical therapists, or clinical social workers), and (vi) applied behavior analysis when provided or supervised by a board certified behavior analyst who shall be licensed by the Board of Medicine. Certain insurers may be exempt from requirements for 1 year and may reapply for the exemption yearly.

Citation: Va. Code Ann. § 38.2-3418.17

West Virginia

Requires health insurance plans issued or renewed after January 1, 2012, to include coverage for diagnosis, evaluation and treatment of autism spectrum disorder in individuals aged eighteen months to eighteen years. The individual must be diagnosed with autism spectrum disorder at age 8 or younger. Treatment shall be determined to be medically necessary by a licensed physician or licensed psychologist.

Note: Speech language services are not clearly defined in the statue. However, applied behavioral analysis is specifically included and coverage limitations are set out.

Citation: W.Va. Code § 5-16B-6e, 33-16-3v, 33-24-7k, 33-25A-8j

Wisconsin

Requires every disability insurance policy, and every self–insured health plan of the state or a county, city, town, village, or school district, to provide coverage for an insured of treatment for the mental health condition of autism spectrum disorder if the treatment is prescribed by a physician and provided by any of the following who are qualified to provide intensive–level services or no intensive–level services: a psychiatrist; a psychologist; a social worker; a paraprofessional working under the supervision of a psychiatrist, psychologist or social worker; a professional working under the supervision of an outpatient mental health clinic; a speech–language pathologist; or an occupational therapist. The coverage required shall provide at least $50,000 for intensive–level services per insured per year, with a minimum of 30 to 35 hours of care per week for a minimum duration of 4 years, and at least $25,000 for no intensive–level services per insured per year.

Citation: Wis. Stat. §632.895(12m)

WWW.Govtrack.US/states/bills/2012

If you do have coverage, watch for limitations, because treatment for autism is so individualized that there are few uniform standards or protocols for insurance companies to follow. That means parents often have to argue that a certain therapy or treatment is necessary. Also, be sure to check any caps on treatment. What may look generous—say $36,000 a year—can be spent quickly. Or there may be limits on how many sessions of a particular type of therapy will be paid for each year.

It is important to coordinate your insurance coverage with the services you may be receiving from your child's school. If an occupational therapist sees your child regularly in school, for example, you may want to save your insurance dollars for other therapies.

In addition, you may need to be especially aggressive about coverage for some medical conditions. Gastrointestinal problems, for instance, are extremely common in autistic children.

The financial aspect of autism is the iceberg under the water. Most parents start to think about early intervention, developmental therapy, and alternative programs in terms of dollars and cents. How much does it cost? Do I have enough? Where can I get extra services at no cost? Lesson learned: do not get too caught in that cycle of thinking about the money. Do not assume that autism treatments are financially prohibitive or impossible! You have options. Check-out the following: Helping Hand, Family First, Aid for Autistic Children Foundation, Mesa Angels, Financial Aid and Medical Assistance for Family of Autistic Children, Modestneeds. org, Autism Assistance Resource Information and Grant for Families living with Autism. You are not alone. I know because I have been there already.

Doctor fees, medical and therapy costs, and co-pays are enough to drive the sanest person crazy. My wife and I are very thrifty, and we still have occasional late nights trying to balance the books and prioritizing what is important. If the funds are not available and you do not have the cash to pay for all the out-of-pocket expenses, get all you can from social services. Even if you think there is no way social services are going to pay for what you need, just ask and then pursue it! It's not what you think; it's what you actually know that counts.

If you have insurance, stay on the phone until you get what you want. Give them grief and be a "bee in their bonnet" until they find a way to pay for your child's needed services. It's common knowledge that insurance companies will squeeze you out of getting a service if you let them. Always use the worst-case scenario to position your child's need for services. They want you to give in and walk away.

Public agencies are there to help. Do not be afraid to demonstrate that your child is in great need. In general, these agencies serve individuals with disabilities who demonstrate a need for those services. All agencies have major and moderate programs that may be appropriate for your child. Some of these programs have income, asset, and other eligibility rules that are important. There are waivers for those making too much money and help for those who do not have the financial means.

Other benefits that will likely become extremely important for adults with disabilities are Social Security Insurance (SSI) payments and your state Medicaid program. These two programs will typically establish a baseline of eligibility for other various educational, housing, and support programs in your state.

Therefore, eligibility for these programs is a gateway to many other benefits. Often when I meet with family members, they may initially feel that they do not need to worry about qualifying for public benefits because they have planned financially and adequately, saved money, for their disabled child. The disabled child has wonderful brothers and sisters who will take care of them. Unfortunately, public benefits are still very important for many people with disabilities for various reasons that may not immediately become apparent.

The following are examples are a baseline to keep in mind:

1. Predicting the cost of your disabled child's future needs is so difficult that saving enough for his or her lifetime is almost impossible. You cannot depend on your other children to support the person with the disability. Too many things can prevent them from doing so, including disability, divorce, creditor issues, and their own or their family's health issues. Some programs depend on public benefits eligibility to enroll, and it may be difficult to pay for those services when your child needs them for personal financial reasons. You may not think your child needs it now. So, take it for later should the need arise for that type of support.

2. You want your child to be declared eligible for benefits under today's eligibility rules because with every year that goes by, the rules makes it harder and harder to qualify. Medicaid is a helpful program for many people with disabilities. It offers care and medical supports that most private insurers do not pay for, such as personal care.

Below are some options for financial support:

Nonprofit and health foundations: There are some organizations, like the private physician's services, which have suspended co-pays for children and families with autism. United HealthCare Children's Foundation provides grants for autism services to middle- and low-income families for treatments such as speech and occupational therapy not provided by school districts or covered by insurance.

Gifts: Ask family members and friends to fund a therapy in lieu of a Christmas or birthday gift they would otherwise give you or your child with autism.

Scholarships and stipends: Some groups, like Special Needs Network, Inc., give special-needs students scholarships and stipends to assist them in transitioning from high school to college or the workplace. The criterion for partial and full scholarships is based on income, with allowances for a number of children and medical bills for child with autism. You must send in the complete scholarship or grant form by the deadline provided. All information that is required must be enclosed with the registration form in order to continue with the process. Finally, the scholarship/grant committee will meet, go over all the information, and will determine if the scholarship/grant will be approved and the amount.

Professional bartering: If you have an expertise in a particular area, such as law, accounting, or dentistry, you can provide services in exchange for therapy services for your child with special needs. You may also work at a therapy clinic and, in lieu of being paid, arrange for your child to receive therapy hours.

Supplemental services: If you have a college student or other interested and available family member, have them take some training on a particular intervention strategy to supplement the professional services your child is receiving. Although not a substitute for a professional, this is a way to extend the learning process at low or no cost to you.

The American Autism Association: will work with parents who are struggling to make ends meet financially by connecting them with funding opportunities to send their children to the very best camps and after-school programs. That means you're not out of pocket or on your own in the quest for affordable, quality care and social support and development for you child.

Non-for-profit: camps and social development organization groups sponsored by corporate donations, private gifts, funding from other sources, and foundations like United Way are a very good resource to tap into. All activities are normally at no cost or a minimal fee for children and adults with autism for food/board and activities. Advancing the public good by enhancing the lives of all people living with multiple disadvantages, including autism, is one of their overarching social goals.

Grants: are available for specific medical needs. The grants are normally $500 or less. This may not seem like a lot, but every little bit adds up when you are at zero, and this money does not have to be paid back. The application process is a bit lengthy, but the money is paid to your provider of services.

The Helping Hand Program: provides families with financial assistance in getting necessary biomedical treatments, supplements, and therapy services for their autistic children. Do not apply for this grant if you are seeking funds for respite care, fencing, trampolines, swing-sets, trips to Disney World, etc. Also be aware that this grant maker will pay your medical provider directly; no funds will come through your hands.

Autism Supports Daily is an organization that uses donor funds to provide financial assistance, support, guidance, recreational activities, and educational training to families and friends of children and young adults with autism spectrum disorder. Grants total no more than $400 per family, and may be limited to the Vermont area (though that information isn't provided on the foundation's Web site).

SEARCHING FOR GRANT OPTIONS

The most important thing you can do when beginning your grant search is to carefully match your project with the grantor's award requirements. For example, if the desired grant is only given to schools in inner cities, only apply if you meet that criterion. Otherwise, you'll be wasting your time. With that in mind, three major sources for grant money exist: federal and state governments, private foundations, and corporations.

Each grant is unique and follows a set of specific rules and differing levels of requirements concerning who can apply, the application process itself, how the money must be spent, and the methods of evaluation, qualifications, and assessment. Most severe cases come first. Our children need to be on that severe list to qualify.

AUTISM 411

HIPAA health-care law prevented a Delaware mother from making psychiatric visits with her eighteen-year old daughter. The mother could not even discuss with the doctors whether or not her daughter was properly medicated, because the daughter was legally considered an adult. When a child turns eighteen, the law and the courts recognize him or her as an adult even if he or she cannot fully function as one.

While privacy is a well-intentioned objective, it can have serious implications for the medical care of individuals with autism. Currently one in five or fifty-four million people in the United States report a disability, and one in nine children under eighteen receive special education services. Therefore, parents should be planning ahead on how they can partake in medical decisions for children with special needs after they turn eighteen.

The number of parents not positioned to take care of

their adult child with autism keeps on growing. It is well documented in the United States and globally that only the reported cases of autism can be statistically verified. Therefore the dollars that could help are not allocated, because unreported cases artificially reduce the impact and extent of autism and available funding sources. Services are provided and put in place based on need. So, if we want more services, we have to demonstrate the extent of the epidemic. The numbers are alarmingly low, while cultural or other social aspects prevent many cases of autism from being reported. The shame factor is still very strong in rural and underdeveloped parts of the world.

If you are feeling at all that your child with special needs may lack significant understanding or capability to make or communicate responsible decisions for him or herself, as related to health-care decisions, plan ahead before you are prevented from participating in critical medical and care decisions. Even under HIPPA, there are steps parents can take to ensure legal access to medical and mental health information about their adult child with special needs.

Parents have three options. They can declare their child to be mentally incompetent when he or she reaches eighteen and assume legal guardianship, seek partial guardianship for medical decisions through obtaining a power of attorney, or secure a release or consent form. Because each family is different, they must choose a solution that best meets their children's needs.

CHAPTER 13:

THE ECONOMICS
OF AUTISM

A n entire generation of young adults with mild or severe autism will be coming into the community or living at home with parents after high school or vocational school. At some point they are going to require additional services from a system that is struggling to meet current needs for services.

It is possible that many will receive partial benefits and not the full benefit of services they expect. This gap will not be driven by the individual's economic status, but by limited historical need for the services being requested. The more demand on the system for these services the more likely resources will be found to support that need. If parents waited until their child is eighteen to claim waivers and other available benefits then the social services budgets are put together on the low end. So there is always more demand and less supply.

For societies and communities that do not have the infrastructure enjoyed at varying degrees by families in the United States, this population will vanish into obscurity as governments see further reductions in their economic advantage and across the board budget cuts affecting the socially most vulnerable including children with autism.

To protect our loved ones with autism, start early, get into the social services system, and build a history for services your child needs and will continue to need as they transition into future services.

This ensures that our loved ones will qualify for new services and or be covered at some level of services is very important. This will be a very different situation for those trying to apply for new services. The future is unknown, and I do not pretend to predict it. This is not the scope of my book. However, just take a look at our global, national and local economies, and how fewer resources are being shifted to home and community based support services. Essentially getting services in a group home or assisted living situation can become very challenging in the future. The level of funding provided in either situation is subject to a countries ability to generate greater tax and other available revenue sources.

The point being made is to encourage parents to secure benefits from all sources as soon as possible.

Procrastination or not seeing the immediate need for it now can impact future benefits and funding levels.

Our children are not just recipients of funds and support services they are consumers of products and other services. The quality of life can also be immensely impacted. About 5.8 million American schoolchildren, ages six to twenty-one, receive special education services through the federal Individuals with Disabilities Education Act.

This growing group of special individuals can be counted on as an economic force of consumption to be reckoned with by the US economy. There will be 5.8 million consumers of durable goods and services including clothing, electronics, toilet paper, soap, fast food, and public transportation. These numbers can be converted into potentially 5.8 million voters, taxpayers, employees/employers, and philanthropists.

These 5.8 million Children and adults with autism contribute to their communities and local jurisdictions by way of sales and use tax (indirect) or income tax (direct).

My point from a purely economic standpoint is that children and adults affected by autism are a force to be reckoned with, especially as economies struggle to grow consumption.

Economies and economists are looking for new ways for every breathing citizen to consume more goods and services, which can help turn the wheels of commerce and rebuild global enterprise. This is an important paradigm shift impacting the special-needs population. This shift in the dynamics of economies is of special importance now more than ever, when looking at funding options and entitlements both public and corporate. Long gone are the days of "handouts" when the autism community was small and insignificant.

In the USA Autism cost for one person on the ASD spectrum is $1.4 Million per year. In total the economic cost of services for autism related treatment and support is in excess of $137 Billion per year. This is more than the Gross Domestic Product of small developing countries. This cost is a target for governments looking for ways to balance their budgets due to lower tax revenues.

It is very important for parents and caregivers to know why social services for the special needs community are being trimmed. Sometimes we complain a lot about what we cannot get. But if the resources are not there, what does plan B look like for our children with special needs. I put less faith in the ability of the government to provide the full spectrum of services that my son will need over a long-term. Even beyond my-lifetime. Having this information helps me with long-term planning for my child with special needs.

This is not an America only problem. Around the world families of children with autism are having the same set of unique challenges. In welfare states, the main costs of autism are generally for living support and daily activities, rather than interventions, which are often state-covered or subsidized. Studies from Great

Britain confirm the lifetime costs of autism. Autism has lifetime consequences, with potentially a range of impacts on the health, wellbeing, social integration and quality of life of individuals and families. Many of those impacts are economic.

> The estimated cost of autism spectrum disorders (ASDs) in the UK is high. Data on prevalence, level of intellectual disability and place of residence were combined with average annual costs of services and support, together with the opportunity costs of lost productivity. The costs of supporting children with ASDs were estimated to be £2.7 billion each year. For adults, these costs amount to £25 billion each year. The lifetime cost, after discounting, for someone with ASD and intellectual disability is estimated at approximately £1.23 million, and for someone with ASD without intellectual disability is approximately £0.80 million.
>
> Knapp, Martin.
> Economic cost of autism in the UK, May 2009

Survey data concerning residential location and schooling in Egypt collectively represent a point of departure from many North American and European countries. In these countries, families of autistic individuals generally have access to and utilize various residential placement options. Autistic school-age children in these countries are generally enrolled in regular or special education schools. In contrast, the Egyptian experience with ASD care appears to be based on a "home-grown" service, whose cost implications substantially differ from those in many developed/industrialized countries, particularly in the western hemisphere.

In the U.S. the Divisions of Developmental Disabilities (DDD) services are dependent on availability of funding and/or eligibility for the specific service. At a defined age previously eligible services become non-eligible as illustrated below.

Developmental Delays, Down Syndrome, Too severe to be assessed, Medically Intensive Children's Program are only covered through ages 0-9. Intellectual Disability (ID), Cerebral Palsy, Epilepsy, Autism, Another Neurological Condition, Other condition similar to ID are covered from 9-18+

The following listing of DDD services can be affected by changes in economic conditions. For planning purposes it is important to know what services the DDD will target for future cuts.

Adult Family Homes: Adult Family Homes are regular neighborhood homes where staff assumes responsibility for the safety and well-being of the adult. A room, meals, laundry, supervision and varying levels of assistance with care are provided. Some provide occasional nursing care. Some offer specialized care for people with mental health issues, developmental disabilities or dementia. The home can have two to six residents and is licensed by the state.

Alternative Living Services: Alternative Living Services are instructional services provided by an individual contractor. The service focuses on community-based individualized training to enable a client to live as independently as possible with minimal residential services.

Companion Homes: Companion Homes provide residential services and supports in an adult foster care model to no more than one adult DDD client. The services are offered in a regular family residence approved by DDD to assure client health, safety, and well-being. DDD reimburses the provider for the instruction and support service. Companion homes provide 24-hour available supervision.

Early Support for Infants and Toddlers (ESIT): Provides early intervention services, including family resources coordination, for eligible children from birth to age 3 and their families

Group Homes: Group Homes are community-based residences serving 2 or more adult clients and are licensed as either a boarding home or an adult family home. Group Homes contract with DDD to provide 24-hour instruction and support. The provider owns or leases the facility. Clients must pay participation for room and board to the service provider.

Intermediate Care Facilities for Individuals with Intellectual Disabilities (ICF/ID):ICF/IDs are residential settings that provide habilitation training, 24-hour supervision, and medical/nursing services for Medicaid eligible clients who are in need of the active treatment services provided in these facilities.

Medically Intensive Children's Program (MICP): MICP provides in-home private duty nursing services to eligible children who have medically intensive needs.

Support Living Services: Supported Living Services offer instruction and support to persons who live in their own homes in the community. Supports may vary from a few hours per month up to 24 hours per day of one-to-one support. Clients pay for their own rent, food, and other personal expenses. DDD contracts with private agencies to provide Supported Living services.

State Operated Living Alternatives (SOLA): SOLA programs offer Supported Living services. SOLA programs are operated by DDD with state employees providing instruction and support to clients.

Voluntary Placement Services (VPS): Voluntary Placement Services offer a variety of supports to eligible children living in a licensed setting outside the family home, when the placement is due solely to the child's disability

Care Providers continue to adjust their quality of services due to economic conditions affecting their ability to operate at a profit. This is a concern for me as a parent looking forward. This is most disturbing if my son should need support from one of these care providers.

Geographic settings (based on urbanization level) affect accessibility and affordability of special needs/ ASD-related facilities. Statistics results segregate by geographic cluster survey data on residential location. Few surveyed families utilized non-household sources of autism care, regardless of geographic setting.

However, families in urban districts were more likely to avail of (scarce) residential placement options, special needs resources, and medical/health care, whether in addition to, or in lieu of, household care for their autistic family members.

I feel strongly that it is important for every father to be very knowledgeable about the services our children will need and how those services will be impacted by economic underfunding from the government or bottom line cost cutting from caregivers servicing our children.

CHAPTER 14:

TRANSITION

T his section of the book is the culmination of all our efforts to develop Aarons potential and capabilities, advocate for all possible services and support that he needs and engaging in early intervention techniques.

Transition refers to a change in status from behaving primarily as a student to assuming emergent adult roles in the community. These roles include employment, participating in post-secondary education, maintaining a home, becoming appropriately involved in the community, and experiencing satisfactory personal and social relationships.

The process of enhancing transition involves the participation and coordination of school programs, youth/adult agency services, and natural supports within the community."

Will Aaron be able to transition into the vocational

training, the world of work and independent living arrangements? Transition opportunities available to Aaron include: Roosevelt Warm Springs and Cave springs vocational training through support of the department of labor. Work support resources for on the job training is also another program offered by the department of labor to help Aaron transition when he gets to that point.

Tommy Nobis provides internship training programs which are fee based. The fees are assessed on the parent's ability to pay or subsidize the fee. Tommy Nobis caters for on-the-job training and development during the summer breaks and weekends from sixteen years old. This is our dream that our son will ultimately be capable of transitioning into these available opportunities. This is the dream of every parent of a child with autism.

Just because an individual has special needs doesn't mean he or she cannot make any decisions on their own. Many People with special needs are high functioning. They live independently from their parents, have jobs, and can tend to basic needs. However, some individuals may need assistance in making certain decisions that require understanding complex information, such as completing tax returns, paying bills, applying for a loan, completing medical forms, etc.

1: Transitioning the special needs community is a social effort. It is in the government through social services, parents and caregivers best interest to help youth with disabilities achieve their maximum potential in adulthood and having an opportunity to be productive members of their communities.

2: Some states have tackled transition needs through a separate line item in their budget. Many state agencies and nonprofit organizations have made achieving successful transitions a priority goal for the next three to five years. Unfortunately, given the current status of the economy and the overwhelming amount of work to be done, we still have a long way to go as a society. Looking at the employment statistics for those with disabilities provides insight into the challenges to transition those with autism and other disabilities into the working environment.

<u>Labor Force Participation</u>
People with disabilities: 20.0%
People without disabilities: 68.9%

<u>Unemployment Rate</u>
People with disabilities: 12.9%
People without disabilities: 8.7%

In order to achieve a successful transition to adulthood, an individual's transition plan must look at many elements of adult living: employment opportunities, vocational and post-secondary education, where to live and with whom, independent living skills, recreation, leisure activities, social relationships, self-advocacy, health and safety, financial benefits, and income planning.

SCHOOL TO WORK

All students with disabilities must operate under an Individualized Education Plan (IEP), which must include a recreation, leisure activities, social relationships, self-advocacy, health and safety, financial benefits, and income planning. Transition planning form by the time the student turns sixteen years of age, in accordance with the Individuals with Disabilities Education Act (IDEA). IDEA states that appropriate educational and transitional services are guaranteed to a child having an IEP.

In order to get the best outcome, the team which includes a caseworker from the department of labor and the teacher must review the student's strengths and preferences. It must be apparent to the team what work related activities the student would probably like and ultimately be successful in. Aaron likes the outdoors and customer service type activities. From that his options can be broadened or narrowed for training and placement opportunities. It all starts with an action plan that discusses instruction, related services, community experiences, employment, daily living skills, and functional vocational evaluations.

Many times parents see a transition planning form that merely repeats the same goals listed in the IEP. This does not really satisfy the requirements for transition planning. Transition goals are separate from IEP goals because they look at more than just the educational process.

This is when a parent's and student's vision

statement, which is a required part of the IEP, becomes very important. A student may state that he wants to be a professional baseball player. Well, not all of us have the skill set to be a professional athlete. But there are ways to include the love of baseball in this student's life and employment plans.

Perhaps the student can volunteer for a local team, or maybe he can work at a sports store or a stadium. Once you have the vision, mapping out the process through individualized assessments and an action plan becomes a little easier.

The actor Cuba Gooding starred in a movie called Radio. He acted the role of an autistic young man, who would always watch the local football team workout. The coach was struck by Radio's dedication. Football coach Harold Jones (Harris) befriends Radio (Gooding), a mentally-challenged man who becomes a student at T.L. Hanna High School in Anderson, South Carolina. Their friendship extends over several decades, where Radio transforms from a shy, tormented man into an inspiration to his community

Our children are endowed with the ability to shine, become their best and an inspiration in their respective communities. This is an opportunity which transition service provides our children through help from the department of labor. Just like Coach Harold Jones, someone is willing to go above and beyond to provide the support and help that my son and your child needs to succeed.

MARSHALING SUPPORT IN THE WORKPLACE

The workplace is the last place most parents will look to for help and support just because they tend to keep private about it. Just look at the amount of hours we spend in an office environment; it is one of the best places to find resources that are designed to help us become productive by giving us the tools needed to support personal and professional needs.

Support is always available at the corporate level for families raising children with challenges and other special needs. Get plugged in to those group meetings. You will be surprised by the resources that are available. These meetings are held periodically and benefit from the shared experience of other parents and outside resources you may not be aware of. Topics are well thought out and are very focused on and relevant to the specific needs of the group participants.

These corporate-sponsored formats also provide peer support for families. Access to resources at work has enabled my family to get at the benefits and information that I can take action on outside the corporate environment.

FINANCIAL MANAGEMENT

In order to stay under these income and asset limits, most special needs planners will use two different kinds of special needs trusts to allow a family or even the disabled persons themselves to put aside resources to help support them and still qualify for public benefits.

These trusts, if appropriately drafted, do not count as assets of the person with the disability. The most popular trust is typically known as a Supplemental Needs Trust (SNT). This trust is funded with other people's money, not money of the person with the disability.

In most instances, the trust is funded at the death of the parents of the disabled person, but may also be funded by the parents during their lifetimes. The trust may also hold gifts from anybody else who would like to provide support for the disabled beneficiary.

This trust is set aside for the benefit of the disabled person and must be completely discretionary. In other words, the trustee has the absolute authority to decide what distributions to make from the trust. The disabled person may not be a trustee. The trust is held for the lifetime of the disabled beneficiary, and the original creators of the trust get to decide who the successor trustees and beneficiaries will be.

In addition to that trust, there is a provision under the Social Security laws that allows disabled people to take their own money and put it in a trust that will be available for their benefit but will not count against them when qualifying for public benefits. This is typically know as a (d)(4)(A) trust or an OBRA 93 trust.

It seems odd that the government would allow this, but there is a catch. If a disabled beneficiary does utilize a trust of this type, when he or she dies, the trust must name as the successor beneficiary each state that has provided Medicaid benefits to the disabled beneficiary.

The state Medicaid agency may recoup or "recover" all costs of providing medical care to that disabled beneficiary for their entire lifetime.

This means that if a person with a disability passes away and there is $100,000 left in the trust, a state may place a lien on those assets to satisfy any medical payments it has made throughout the person's lifetime. In addition, there are other significant differences Between a (d)(4)(A) and an SNT. A (d)(4)(A) trust can only be established by a parent, grandparent, legal guardian of the disabled beneficiary, or by court order.

The trust can only be established and funded for a person under the age of sixty-five years. Lastly, the trust must be irrevocable, meaning it cannot be changed or terminated. Although these requirements can be very daunting, a (d) (4)(A) trust is very helpful to a person with a disability under certain circumstances so that they do not lose valuable benefits provided by the federal or state government. The kinds of circumstances that impact the trust and can involve actions by social security to reduce benefits to offset income directly received by the trust beneficiary are as follows:

1. estate planning mistakes resulting in money left directly to the individual with disabilities;
2. receipt of child or adult support payments;
3. settlements from accident or other civil tort claims; and
4. Lottery winnings.

LEGAL AUTHORITIES

The last area reviewed when meeting with a family of a transitioning disabled youth is whether the parents or other trusted adults need to remain involved in some legal capacity with the person with the disability.

This could include guardianship, conservatorship, or durable powers of attorney and health-care proxies. When people turn eighteen years old, they reach the age of majority and become their own person.

Regardless of how severe a person's disability is, there is no presumption of incapacity.

Only a court can determine whether a person is incapacitated, to what extent, whether a guardian should be named, and who should be named. This action does not take place automatically; it must be initiated by some interested person.

Each state requires a medical documentation of the incapacity and sets its own standard for determining whether incapacity exists. The most important fact for family members to remember is that without this legal finding of incapacity, there are confidentiality issues around health care and financial information of the disabled person.

Parents can no longer automatically make health-care decisions or perform banking tasks for their child. It often comes as quite a shock to family members when they realize this fact. In order to decide whether guardianship or other legal authorities are appropriate, you must review your child's individual needs, strengths, weaknesses, and risks. Considering whether guardianship can be avoided is a valuable process. Guardianship can be a cumbersome and expensive process. In most states the process is public, meaning it happens in open court, and the pleadings, except for medical information, filed with the court are open to the public.

The legal determination of incapacity eviscerates the option of self-determination. Other alternatives to guardianship such as health-care proxies, powers of attorney, and other agency appointments are less intrusive and should be reviewed.

The statistics of financial and physical abuse and neglect of the disabled in our communities are frightening. Many of our disabled family members may be vulnerable and at risk. Sometimes, protection is needed for the disabled individual by court intervention and oversight.

Perhaps he or she lacks the capacity to validly execute a durable power of attorney or health-care proxy. Or, in rare cases, a court appointed fiduciary is needed because there is no interested party available to serve as an agent under a durable power of attorney or a health-care proxy.

Each state has its own laws regarding health-care proxies and durable powers of attorney, but in general the documents are as follows:

Durable Power of Attorney: governs financial decisions; gives the agent the authority to act on the part of the principal (the person with the disability); it is typically a concurrent power, meaning that the agent and the principal can act simultaneously; cannot be used to void contracts; and is easily revoked by the principal.

Health-Care Proxy: governs health-care decisions; gives the agent the authority to act on the part of the principal; is typically a springing power which goes into effect only when the physician says so; cannot be used for day to day health-care decisions; and can be easily revoked by the principal.

Under each of these documents, the principal has a very low threshold for capacity to sign the documents. He or she must only understand at a very basic level the authority and to whom it is being given. The difficult aspect of this for many people I work with is the fact that it is easily revoked. If you have a child who is variable in any way, this may not be the solution for you.

In Closing

It was a devastating experience for our first child to be diagnosed with autism. This development really took us by surprise; we were unorganized and ill prepared. Shock was eventually superseded by our tireless effort to understand what we needed to do, and do it, while educating ourselves in the process.

There is no parent's "beginner's guide to autism," so it naturally becomes a self-taught, figuring-it-out-as-you-go type of situation. Families are coping under tremendous strain to be the best for their children with autism by loving them unconditionally and working around the clock to give them a fighting chance at a life that is filled with opportunities, comfortable, fruitful, and fulfilling.

I was so eager to do everything possible all at once to position my son for a future that is brighter than his past. I didn't care about the money or the effort; I just wanted to propel things forward. I soon learned that timing is everything. But would I have done things differently? Not really! The success that we have experienced is a direct result of the consistent and continuous repetitive learning and development process.

Looking for answers and support to help me make good decisions that I could live with was like searching for a needle in a haystack. I knew that help had to be somewhere; it was just hard to find it. The experience was painful and frustrating, but insightful as my wife and I worked our way through the maze of appointments, disappointments, information, and misinformation.

Now I understand that fighting for an autistic child's right for help and support is a journey that becomes hard to plan and harder to pursue on your own. Networking with parents having similar experiences is a great resource to identify the shortcuts and issues, which without proper guidance my wife and I were destined to come up against. Other parents are definitely a beginner's resource for how to get the best results with limited experience. At first we kept ourselves so busy doing everything that we didn't have time to network and meet other families; but when we started doing that, it paid off tenfold with the help and advice we received.

Today the journey that started out as a hopeless and monumental task has morphed into a success story exemplified by the progress our son has made over the years. We are so thankful and grateful for every bit of help, advice, and support that has fallen to us along the way.

Overall, the journey has been a bittersweet experience

for our family. We have not arrived yet! However, we have seen big improvements and changes that we once only dreamed were possible. Our son has a chance to live his American dream while embracing a sense of hope for and pride in his future. Thus we have made a very conscious decision to be a resource to other parents of children and adults with autism. We try to make the journey a little better than what we had to endure when we first started. And that is the purpose of this book.

We have many interesting experiences and war stories to share; however, we prefer to temper this with positive and inspiring success stories to prove that this journey can be very rewarding when, all things considered, we have made progress. It's important to put everything that has happened into the correct perspective. I discovered very quickly that while looking for answers and solutions, no father wants to make a bad decision that impacts his child. Sometimes tough decisions have to be made to help Aaron later on in life.

These decisions may appear to be insensitive and harsh at the beginning but it is the end that counts. Inaction is a way to ensure prolonged embarrassing situations. There was a time when I didn't know what I was doing. I just went with the flow for peace sake and the results justified the lack of effort. A colleague used to tell me that you get what you inspect not what you expect!

Trying to mitigate bad experiences and risk along

this journey caused me many sleepless nights and long days. We made many mistakes and bad decisions. But it was part of the overall learning experience. We all just had to get comfortable with it and move forward. Today we are at a better place.

Like many parents of children with autism, we have been told that "autism is tragic." I can say with humble pride that our son is funny, kind, considerate, respectful, smart, and determined. He has overcome some of the most challenging situations facing a child or young adult at this stage of his life. The balanced view is that we have encountered thorny challenges, failures, opportunities, and successes at every stage of our son's life. He is both courageous and brave as he works through his daily challenges to be the best he can be. Sometimes I wish I could take his place and do it all for him. However, I realize there is no long-term benefit in that approach.

Living with autism in our family has given me a "huge moment" to reflect on what is important and what my values really are. Being connected to people and communities, following a passion, and discovering new ways to stay optimistic about the future are the things I feel great pride about. I feel empowered through autism, and sharing with my son these life-learned values is the best possible example and legacy that I can give him. The euphoria experienced after overcoming these hurdles and challenges is beyond words.

Decisions continue to be made and adjusted

periodically through advanced preparation as it relates to education, employment, independent living, and giving serious thought to what needs to be done in the event we are not around anymore. Planning requires time, resources, and support people on our team. The process around transitioning decisions for a child with autism at around age 17 can be the hardest work ever. The plan should be flexible and evolve over time. An attorney specializing in this field, a financial planner, and a care manager can add enormous value when planning for the transition to adulthood for a youth with autism disabilities.

Children and persons with autism face major challenges associated with stigma and discrimination, as well as a lack of access to support. Many struggle with multiple barriers in their daily lives. Far too many suffer terrible discrimination, abuse, and isolation, in violation of their fundamental human rights, as underlined by Ban Ki-moon, General Secretary of the United Nations.

Take the Quiz

How well are you planning for your child's future?

- Do you or your spouse have a vision of how your dependent with autism will live after you are not around anymore?
- Have you identified a guardian, conservator, or a trustee for your dependent?
- Do you have complete understanding of supplementary security income or social-security disability insurance or other government benefits?
- Have you begun the process of setting aside money for your dependent with special needs?
- Do you have a written letter of intent?
- Do you have a special-needs or supplementary-needs trust established to preserve government benefits?
- Have provisions been made to fund these trusts with assets or insurance?
- Have you coordinated your special needs planning with other relatives?

- Have you done everything possible to protect your dependent's financial future?
- Have you planned where your special-needs dependent will live if you are not around any longer?
- Will your dependent be able to earn enough money to care of their needs?
- Will your dependent have adequate health insurance?

OTHER NEED-TO-KNOW AUTISM FACTS AND TIDBITS

- How to Select a Service Coordinator: Useful information and questions to ask to help you select the right service coordinator for your loved one. A service coordinator or case manager assists a person with a developmental disability to develop an individualized plan of service or ISP.

- Respite Services give families time away from taking care of their family member who has a disability. Respite allows family members to go shopping, attend a wedding or funeral, or to just relax and stay at home.

- Suggestions and Tips to Recruit In-Home Respite Providers from where to look for staff to salary.

- Transition Planning: Your child's school district Special Education Department or Committee is required by both federal and state regulations before age level fourteen to begin to help you and your child develop a transition plan from school to life after school—meeting with you, your child, and community agencies to discuss what skills and knowledge your child will need as an adult.

- <u>Person-Centered Planning</u> consists of service options that are based on the choices, strength, and needs of someone who has a developmental disability, rather than a set choice of options for services.

- <u>Supports Intensity Scale:</u> A planning tool designed to measure the level of support that each person with autism and other developmental disabilities need to fully participate in the community.

- <u>Self-Determination</u> is the right of persons with disabilities to make choices about their own lives, to have the same rights and responsibilities as everyone else, and to speak and advocate for themselves.

- <u>Self-Advocacy:</u> Parents are their children's best advocate. However, it is very important for able adults with autism and other developmental disabilities to learn how to advocate and speak up.

- <u>Circle of Support:</u> A group of people interested in getting together to assist a focal person enhance and expand his or her life by helping to reach key personal goals.

- Residential Placement: There are various types of residential placement options available for an individual with autism depending upon the level of care a person may need. This page also offers dozens of valid questions to help you select a residential service provider, as well as an agency interested in providing support and residential opportunity for your loved one.

- Guardianship: A parent is considered by law, the natural guardian of his or her child until that child reaches the age of eighteen. Once the child reaches the age of eighteen, however, a parent or sibling (or other potential guardian) must petition the court to grant guardianship status over the said adult with disabilities.

- Supplemental Needs Trust: Individuals with mental retardation and/or developmental disabilities who have assets over approximately $2,000 are ineligible to receive state and federal services, i.e., HCBS waivers and must spend their money down to this amount first. However, the government does allow "special needs trust" to be set up for children with disabilities.

Special Diet

Autism and a healthy diet work wonders! You are what you eat! From an early age our son would only drink water and consumed a tremendous amount of fruit. He has now acquired the taste for hamburger so it becomes harder to have him eat his vegetables in a normal meal sitting. A good diet has helped with managing certain behaviors that became harder to control. These behaviors interfered with his development at school and other social settings with kids and adults.

I was given a meal chart by an endocrinologist. The meal chart sat on the refrigerator for two months until one day I decided to read and apply the daily suggested intake of fruit, protein, and vegetables. I noticed that when we regimentally followed the dietary plan, some significant changes started to take place in Aaron, related to a calmer presence and better concentration after three months. Today he drinks lemonade and fruit juice but no soda, and his fast-food preference is chicken nuggets and chicken sandwiches. Eating right and sensibly does wonders for us as adults, and well-structured diets have had the same benefits and similar outcomes for our child with autism.

Fried food in his diet is limited to French fries and maybe the occasional fried chicken legs. Foods with high fat content are kept to a minimum. He has his favorite restaurants that he frequently visits. However, the balance between alternative food choices is always maintained. Less sugar, salt, fat, artificial colorings, and all those ingredients on the label that no one can pronounce correctly are limited in his daily intake.

Now he eats a good balance among the available food choices independently and on his own. The results are outstanding. Drinking large amounts of water also helps to relieve the body of toxins that my son was reacting to in a negative way, which finally ended up being demonstrated in his performance and behavior.

The entire experience can only be expressed as awesome! I am very humbled to be in a position to share our story and experiences, with the hope and belief that other parents may find strength and courage in a time of uncertainty. The beginning does not define the end.

I continue to use this material as a reference point for myself first. If the information from this resource can help another family, I have accomplished our shared family goal, to make this journey easier, and a better experience for other families of children and adults with autism.

Quotes to Live By

The following is a selection of personal quotes that have helped to inspire our family and keep us focused when it was extremely difficult.

It is essential that information about the complex difficulties faced by persons with autism and their families on a daily basis is shared in order to ensure a better future for them.
—Evelyne Friedel, President of Autism-Europe

Every day you may make progress. Every step may be fruitful. Yet there will stretch out before you an ever-lengthening, ever-ascending, ever-improving path. You know you will never get to the end of the journey. But this, so far from discouraging, only adds to the joy and glory of the climb.
—Sir Winston Churchill

It's not enough that we do our best; sometimes we have to do what's required.
—Sir Winston Churchill

It is a mistake to try to look too far ahead. The chain of destiny can only be grasped one link at a time.
—Sir Winston Churchill

Success is the ability to go from one failure to another with no loss of enthusiasm.
—Sir Winston Churchill

The ultimate measure of a man is not where he stands in moments of comfort and convenience, but where he stands at times of challenge and controversy.
—Martin Luther King, Jr.

Grant me the serenity to accept the things I cannot change, courage to change the things I can, and wisdom to know the difference!
—Author Unknown

We are what we repeatedly do. Excellence, then, is not an act, but a habit.
—Aristotle

BIBLIOGRAPHY

Knapp, Martin. "Economic cost of autism in the UK."
London School of Economics. May 2009

WORKS CITED

github.com/govtrack/govtrack.us-web

ABOUT THE AUTHOR

Keith Ambersley is a father of a special-needs son diagnosed with pervasive developmental disorder, cognitive impairment, and attention deficit disorder.

In Autism: Turning On the Light, Keith shares his experience with autism, which has developed into a remarkable father-son relationship filled with surprises, passion, rejection, hope, and personal transformation in his thinking. Keith and his family continue to work tirelessly to identify opportunities which transform autism into a gift of hope that can be exchanged with other fathers, parents and caregivers.

Keith and his family live in Marietta, Georgia.